THE AUSTRALIAN
Women's Weekly

EAT CLEAN *with*
SUPERFOODS

THE AUSTRALIAN WOMEN'S WEEKLY
TRIPLE TESTED
TEST KITCHEN

PUBLISHED IN 2016 BY BAUER MEDIA BOOKS, AUSTRALIA.
BAUER MEDIA BOOKS IS A DIVISION OF BAUER MEDIA PTY LTD.

BAUER MEDIA BOOKS

PUBLISHER
JO RUNCIMAN

EDITORIAL & FOOD DIRECTOR
PAMELA CLARK

DIRECTOR OF SALES, MARKETING & RIGHTS
BRIAN CEARNES

ART DIRECTOR & DESIGNER
HANNAH BLACKMORE

SENIOR EDITOR
STEPHANIE KISTNER

OPERATIONS MANAGER
DAVID SCOTTO

FOOD EDITOR
LOUISE PATNIOTIS

RECIPE DEVELOPERS
CHARLOTTE BINNS-MCDONALD,
TESSA IMMENS, KIRSTEN JENKINS,
ANGELA DEVLIN, ALEXANDRA ELLIOTT,
ELIZABETH MACRI, SHARON KENNEDY,
REBECCA TRUDA

PHOTOGRAPHER
JAMES MOFFATT

STYLISTS
SOPHIA YOUNG, OLIVIA BLACKMORE,
ANNETTE FORREST

PHOTOCHEF
ANGELA DEVLIN

PRINTED IN CHINA
BY LEO PAPER PRODUCTS LTD

TITLE EAT CLEAN WITH SUPERFOODS /
PAMELA CLARK
ISBN 978-1-74245-712-3 (PAPERBACK)
NOTES INCLUDES INDEX
SUBJECTS COOKING (NATURAL FOODS).
NATURAL FOODS. HEALTH.
OTHER CREATORS/CONTRIBUTORS:
CLARK, PAMELA.
ALSO TITLED AUSTRALIAN WOMEN'S WEEKLY.
DEWEY NUMBER: 641.5637

© BAUER MEDIA PTY LIMITED 2016
ABN 18 053 273 546

PUBLISHED BY BAUER MEDIA BOOKS,
A DIVISION OF BAUER MEDIA PTY LTD,
54 PARK ST, SYDNEY; GPO BOX 4088,
SYDNEY, NSW 2001, AUSTRALIA
PH +61 2 9282 8618; FAX +61 2 9126 3702
WWW.AWWCOOKBOOKS.COM.AU

ORDER BOOKS
PHONE 136 116 (WITHIN AUSTRALIA)

OR ORDER ONLINE AT
WWW.AWWCOOKBOOKS.COM.AU

SEND RECIPE ENQUIRIES TO
RECIPEENQUIRIES@BAUER-MEDIA.COM.AU

CONNECT WITH US

 FACEBOOK.COM/
AWWCOOKBOOKS

 INSTAGRAM
@AWWCOOKBOOKS

 PINTEREST
AWWCOOKBOOKS

 YOUTUBE
AUSTRALIANWOMENSWEEKLYCOOKBOOKS

EAT CLEAN *with*
SUPERFOODS

THE AUSTRALIAN WOMEN'S WEEKLY

TRIPLE TESTED

TEST KITCHEN

CONTENTS

REAL FOOD with POWER

In the modern world where diets seem to be all about weight loss, it's easy to forget that we all need to eat really well to optimally nourish our bodies, boost vitality and give us the best chance of great health.

This is where superfoods come in. Rather than turning to supplements (although these have their place), you are almost always better to consume the foods that provide these nutrients. In part this is because nature provides a wonderful balance and package of nutrients not found in individual supplements. In addition plant foods provide a wealth of phytochemicals – substances such as antioxidants that benefit us enormously, way beyond our basic needs for vitamins and minerals.

While there is no official definition of a superfood, the word is used to describe foods and drinks that are the star players in providing these nutrients and phytochemicals. A superfood might be high in one particular nutrient, such as oysters for their outstanding zinc content. Alternatively it may have a high level of a phytonutrient known to be beneficial in protecting against a particular disease. Tomatoes are a good example as they provide a rich source of lycopene shown to reduce the risk of prostate cancer in men. Other superfoods boast an army of protective phytochemicals and nutrients: Nuts are nutritional powerhouses providing many nutrients including fibre, folate, magnesium, vitamin E, riboflavin, calcium and protein, along with a collection of different antioxidants. Extra virgin olive oil contains not just healthy, stable monounsaturated fat, but also has vitamin E, at least 29 polyphenols (known to be protective in the body), a chemical called squalene that plays a role in protecting your skin from the sun, and something called oleocanthal that is anti-inflammatory. You can see that foods such as these have something extra to offer us and are truly deserving of superfood status.

The best news is that superfoods do not have to be expensive or exotic. While there are certainly some really interesting superfoods that are imported from other areas of the world, including some of the berries like acai and goji, there are even more superfoods produced locally and available in your local grocer, fishmonger, butcher or supermarket. Locally grown berries, broccoli, cabbage, watercress, Asian greens, mushrooms, seeds, oats, salmon, herring, mussels, game meats, green tea and natural yoghurt are just a few of the foods I certainly classify as superfoods. I particularly love these options as we can all work them more easily into our weekly menus. Look for budget friendly superfoods too; canned salmon or mackerel, frozen berries, canned legumes and packets of whole grains all help to make the family weekly budget go further.

This book is designed to help all of us get more superfoods on our plate to nutrient boost our diets. The end result is so worthwhile. When you and your family eat well you'll feel more energetic, you'll radiate better health and you'll give your body the best protection you can against lifestyle-related diseases. Above all we hope this book will inspire you to broaden the array of foods that you and your family consume, all put together in the most delicious, but completely doable way. Healthy eating has never tasted so good!

Dr Joanna McMillan
Accredited Practising Dietitian & Nutritionist
www.drjoanna.com.au | www.getlean.com.au

TOP 40 SUPERFOODS

POMEGRANATES
FREEKEH
BLUEBERRIES
QUINOA
SALMON
KUMARA
WATERCRESS
ALMONDS & WALNUTS
RASPBERRIES
AVOCADO
TOMATOES
OATS
BEANS & LENTILS
WHITE FISH
BROCCOLI
LEAN RED MEAT
YOGHURT
LINSEEDS
RED/GREEN CABBAGE
CITRUS FRUITS
CHIA SEEDS
KALE
EGGS
HERBS
CAPSICUM
SPINACH & SILVER BEET
PASSIONFRUIT
GARLIC
MANGO
GOJI & ACAI BERRIES
MUSHROOMS
CHICKEN
KIWIFRUIT
ROCKET
MILK
CHILLI

SUPER STARTS

WHETHER IT'S A SMOOTHIE, PANCAKES, OMELETTE OR PORRIDGE, A BREAKFAST HIGH IN PROTEIN, LOW GI AND PACKED WITH ANTIOXIDANTS, VITAMINS AND MINERALS WILL GIVE YOU A MUCH NEEDED MORNING BOOST.

WASH THE KALE LEAVES WELL AND REMOVE THE STEMS BEFORE SHREDDING. FOR A CREAMIER SMOOTHIE, USE FROZEN RIPE BANANAS AND HAVE ALL THE INGREDIENTS COLD.

KALE *And* BANANA

2 MEDIUM RIPE BANANAS (400G)

2 CUPS (60G) SHREDDED KALE LEAVES

1 MEDIUM AVOCADO (250G), CHOPPED

1½ TABLESPOONS HONEY

2 CUPS (500ML) WATER

2 TEASPOONS LINSEEDS

CRUSHED ICE, TO SERVE

1 Place banana, kale, avocado, honey, the water and linseeds in a high powdered juice blender; blend until smooth.

2 Pour smoothie into glasses filled with crushed ice; serve immediately.

prep time 5 minutes **serves** 4 (makes 1 litre)

nutritional count per serving 10.2g total fat (2.1g saturated fat); 804kJ (192 cal); 21.7g carbohydrate; 2.4g protein; 3.5g fibre

I AM
HIGH FIBRE
HIGH IN CALCIUM
LOW FAT

TO REMOVE POMEGRANATE SEEDS, CUT POMEGRANATE IN HALF CROSSWAYS; HOLD IT, CUT-SIDE DOWN, IN THE PALM OF YOUR HAND OVER A BOWL, THEN HIT THE OUTSIDE FIRMLY WITH A WOODEN SPOON. THE SEEDS SHOULD FALL OUT EASILY; DISCARD ANY WHITE PITH THAT FALLS OUT WITH THEM.

CHIA BIRCHER
with GRANOLA and POMEGRANATE

160G (5 OUNCES) RASPBERRIES

2 CUPS (560G) LOW-FAT GREEK-STYLE YOGHURT

¼ CUP (40G) WHITE CHIA SEEDS

½ TEASPOON VANILLA EXTRACT

1 TABLESPOON PURE MAPLE SYRUP

¾ CUP (60G) TRADITIONAL ROLLED OATS

½ CUP (40G) SLICED RAW ALMONDS

¼ TEASPOON GROUND CINNAMON

1 MEDIUM POMEGRANATE (320G), SEEDS REMOVED (SEE ABOVE)

1 Reserve 12 of the raspberries. Mash remaining raspberries in a medium bowl with yoghurt until combined. Add chia seeds, extract and 2 teaspoons of the maple syrup. Cover; refrigerate overnight.

2 Preheat oven to 200°C/400°F.

3 Place oats on an oven tray. Bake for 5 minutes or until lightly browned. Add almonds, cinnamon and remaining maple syrup; mix well. Bake for another 5 minutes or until nuts are golden. Cool.

4 Spoon half the yoghurt mixture into four 1 cup (250ml) jars. Top with half the pomegranate seeds and granola. Repeat layering with remaining yoghurt mixture, pomegranate seeds and granola. Serve topped with reserved raspberries.

prep + cook time 25 minutes (+ refrigeration) **serves** 4

nutritional count per serving 18.7g total fat (5.8g saturated fat); 1849kJ (442 cal); 48g carbohydrate; 13.5g protein; 11.5g fibre

tip Make a double batch of the granola and store in an airtight container for up to 1 week.

APPLE PIE PANCAKES

WITH BLACKBERRY COMPOTE

1 CUP (135G) FROZEN BLACKBERRIES

⅓ CUP (80ML) PURE MAPLE SYRUP

1 CUP (150G) WHOLEMEAL SPELT FLOUR

2 TEASPOONS BAKING POWDER

1 TEASPOON GROUND CINNAMON

½ TEASPOON MIXED SPICE

1 CUP (250ML) BUTTERMILK

1 FREE-RANGE EGG, BEATEN LIGHTLY

2 TEASPOONS VANILLA EXTRACT

1 MEDIUM PINK LADY APPLE (150G), UNPEELED, GRATED COARSELY

MICRO MINT, TO SERVE

1 Combine blackberries and half the maple syrup in a small saucepan; bring to the boil. Reduce heat; simmer, stirring occasionally, for 10 minutes or until berries soften. Remove from heat; cool.

2 Sift flour, baking powder, cinnamon, mixed spice and a pinch of salt into a medium bowl; gradually whisk in combined buttermilk, egg, extract and remaining maple syrup until batter is smooth. Fold in apple.

3 Heat an oiled, medium non-stick frying pan over medium heat. Pour ¼-cup of batter for each pancake into pan; cook until bubbles appear on the surface. Turn; cook until browned lightly. Remove from pan; cover to keep warm. Repeat with remaining batter to make a total of eight pancakes.

4 Serve pancakes with blackberry compote and mint.

prep + cook time 35 minutes (+ cooling) **serves** 4
nutritional count per serving 3.5g total fat (1.4g saturated fat); 1271kJ (303 cal); 50.5g carbohydrate; 10.3g protein; 6.7g fibre
tip You could use frozen mixed berries instead of blackberries.

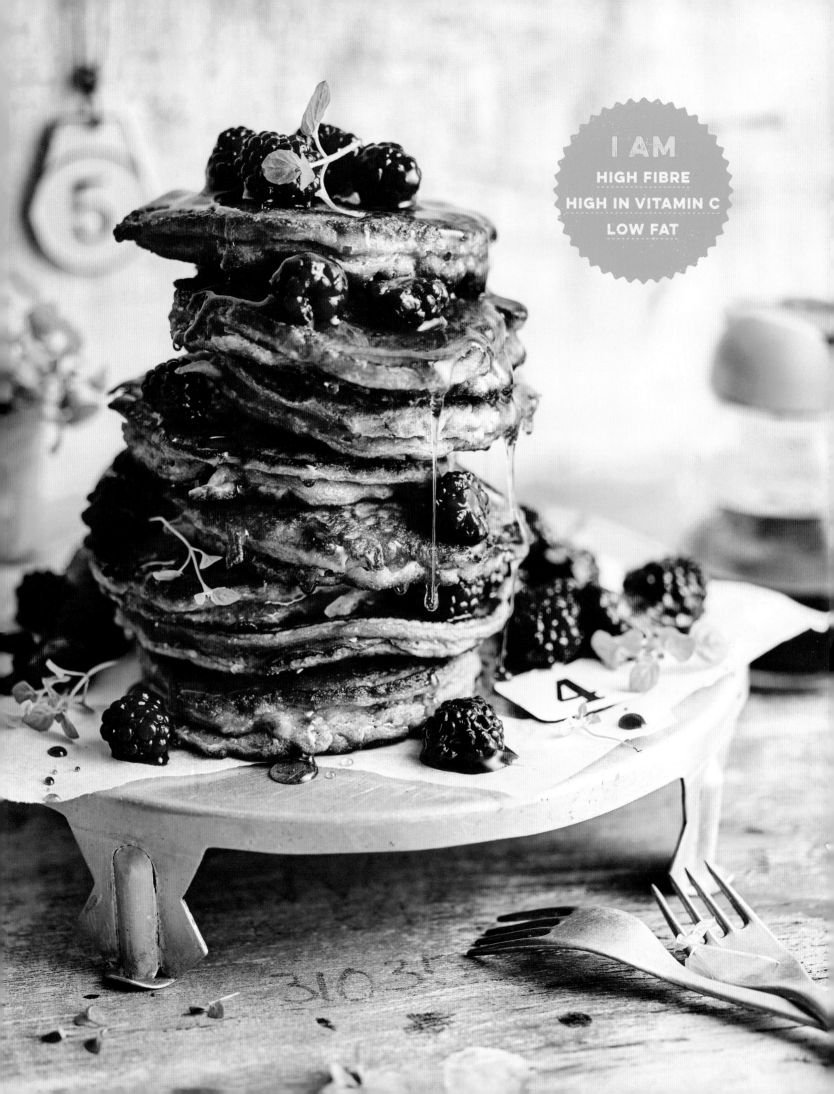

I AM
VEGETARIAN
RICH IN VITAMINS
LOW CARB

CAVOLO NERO FRITTERS
WITH PICKLED BEETROOT

3 LARGE ZUCCHINI (450G), GRATED COARSELY

1 TEASPOON SALT

3 CAVOLO NERO (TUSCAN CABBAGE) LEAVES (30G), TRIMMED, SHREDDED FINELY

2 TABLESPOONS CHOPPED FRESH MINT LEAVES

¼ CUP (40G) WHOLEMEAL PLAIN (ALL-PURPOSE) FLOUR

2 CLOVES GARLIC, CRUSHED

2 FREE-RANGE EGGS, BEATEN LIGHTLY

2 TABLESPOONS OLIVE OIL

3 SMALL BEETROOT (BEETS) (300G), PEELED, SLICED THINLY (SEE TIPS)

2 TABLESPOONS CIDER VINEGAR

100G (3 OUNCES) FETTA, CRUMBLED

¼ CUP FRESH MINT LEAVES

2 TABLESPOONS SUNFLOWER SEEDS, TOASTED

HONEY DRESSING

2 TABLESPOONS EXTRA VIRGIN OLIVE OIL

1 TABLESPOON CIDER VINEGAR

½ TEASPOON HONEY

1 Combine zucchini and salt in a colander; stand in the sink for 10 minutes to drain. Using your hands, squeeze excess liquid from zucchini. Place zucchini in a medium bowl with cavolo nero, mint, flour, garlic and egg; season. Mix well to combine.

2 Heat oil in a large non-stick frying pan over medium heat. Pour ¼-cups of mixture into pan, flatten slightly; cook for 5 minutes each side or until golden and crisp. Drain on paper towel; cover to keep warm. Repeat with remaining mixture to make a total of eight fritters.

3 Meanwhile, combine beetroot and vinegar in a bowl; season. Stand for 5 minutes. Drain; reserve pickling liquid for honey dressing.

4 Make honey dressing.

5 Arrange fritters, beetroot, fetta and mint on serving plate. Serve drizzled with dressing and sprinkled with sunflower seeds.

honey dressing Whisk ingredients with reserved pickling liquid in a small bowl until combined.

prep + cook time 35 minutes (+ standing & cooling)

serves 4

nutritional count per serving 28.4g total fat (7.7g saturated fat); 1563kJ (373 cal); 15g carbohydrate; 12g protein; 5.5g fibre

tips Use a mandoline or V-slicer to slice the beetroot very thinly. Cooked fritters can be frozen; reheat for a quick breakfast option.

CHICKPEA PANCAKE
with FRIED EGGS And CHERRY TOMATOES

⅔ CUP (100G) CHICKPEA FLOUR (BESAN)

½ TEASPOON GROUND CUMIN

¾ CUP (180ML) WATER

1 TABLESPOON OLIVE OIL

1 EGG WHITE

1 TABLESPOON OLIVE OIL, EXTRA

170G (5½ OUNCES) ASPARAGUS, TRIMMED

1 CLOVE GARLIC, CHOPPED

250G (8 OUNCES) MIXED CHERRY TOMATOES, HALVED

1 TABLESPOON RED WINE VINEGAR

4 FREE-RANGE EGGS

1 Preheat oven to 180°C/350°F.

2 Place chickpea flour and cumin in a medium bowl; season. Whisk in the water and oil until batter is smooth.

3 Beat egg white in a small bowl with an electric mixer until soft peaks form; gently fold into batter.

4 Heat an oiled 24cm (9½-inch) ovenproof non-stick frying pan over medium heat. Pour batter into pan; cook for 2 minutes or until bubbles form around the edge. Transfer pan to oven; bake for 7 minutes or until pancake is cooked through and light and fluffy.

5 Meanwhile, heat half the extra oil in a large non-stick frying pan over medium heat; cook asparagus for 5 minutes, turning, or until lightly browned and cooked. Remove from pan; keep warm.

6 Add garlic to same pan; cook, stirring for 30 seconds or until fragrant. Add tomatoes and vinegar; cook, breaking tomatoes with the back of a wooden spoon, for 5 minutes or until tomatoes have just broken down. Season. Remove from pan; wipe pan with paper towel.

7 Heat remaining oil in same pan over medium heat. Add eggs; cook for 4 minutes or until whites are set and yolks remain runny.

8 Cut pancake into wedges. Serve wedges topped with fried egg, tomato mixture and asparagus.

prep + cook time 30 minutes (+ cooling) **serves** 4
nutritional count per serving 15.3g total fat (3g saturated fat); 1073kJ (256 cal); 13.7g carbohydrate; 13.6g protein; 4.5g fibre
tip Pancake is best made just before serving.

I AM

VEGETARIAN

PROTEIN RICH

LOW CARB

I AM
VEGETARIAN
ANTIOXIDANTS
LOW FAT

MICROWAVING THE COUSCOUS AFTER IT HAS ABSORBED
THE WATER PRODUCES A LOVELY LIGHT COUSCOUS.

SPICED COUSCOUS
with PASSIONFRUIT YOGHURT

1 CUP (200G) WHOLEMEAL COUSCOUS

2 TEASPOONS EXTRA VIRGIN OLIVE OIL

1 TEASPOON MIXED SPICE

¼ TEASPOON ALLSPICE

¼ CUP (90G) HONEY

1 CUP (250ML) BOILING WATER

½ CUP (50G) WALNUTS, TOASTED

¾ CUP (200G) GREEK-STYLE YOGHURT

2 TABLESPOONS PASSIONFRUIT PULP

2 MEDIUM ORANGES (480G), PEELED, SLICED THINLY

⅓ CUP (50G) BLUEBERRIES

¼ CUP FRESH MINT LEAVES

1 Combine couscous, oil, mixed spice, allspice, a pinch of salt, honey and the boiling water in a medium heatproof bowl; stand for 5 minutes or until liquid is absorbed, fluffing with a fork occasionally.

2 Cover couscous with plastic wrap. Microwave on HIGH (100%) for 30 seconds; fluff couscous with a fork to separate grains. Repeat process two or three times or until couscous is very fluffy. Stir in walnuts.

3 Meanwhile, combine yoghurt and passionfruit in a small bowl.

4 Serve couscous topped with orange slices, blueberries, yoghurt mixture and mint.

prep + cook time 25 minutes **serves** 4

nutritional count per serving 14.6g total fat (2.8g saturated fat); 1993kJ (476 cal); 73.7g carbohydrate; 11g protein; 4.4g fibre

THE QUINOA MIXTURE THICKENS AS IT COOLS, SO ADD MORE COCONUT MILK OR WATER IF YOU WISH TO THIN IT DOWN. WHEN MANGOES ARE NOT IN SEASON, USE PEARS, APPLES OR BANANAS. USE DAIRY-FREE CHOCOLATE, IF YOU PREFER.

COCONUT And MANGO
BREAKFAST BOWL

1 CUP (200G) WHITE QUINOA

1 LITRE (4 CUPS) COCONUT MILK

1 CUP (250ML) WATER

⅓ CUP (55G) COCONUT SUGAR

¼ TEASPOON SEA SALT

¼ CUP (25G) FINELY GRATED DARK CHOCOLATE (70% - 85% COCOA SOLIDS)

2 TABLESPOONS MACADAMIAS, ROASTED, CHOPPED COARSELY

2 TABLESPOONS ALMONDS, ROASTED, CHOPPED COARSELY

2 SMALL MANGOES (600G), SLICED THINLY

¼ CUP FRESH MINT LEAVES, TO SERVE

1 Combine quinoa, coconut milk, the water, half the coconut sugar and the salt in a medium saucepan over high heat; bring to the boil. Reduce heat to low; simmer, covered, for 30 minutes or until quinoa is tender.

2 Serve quinoa mixture topped with remaining coconut sugar, then chocoloate, nuts, mango and mint.

prep + cook time 40 minutes **serves** 4

nutritional count per serving 64.6g total fat (47.5g saturated fat); 3896kJ (931 cal); 71g carbohydrate; 14.4g protein; 9.8g fibre

I AM
HIGH IN FOLATE
HIGH IN VITAMIN C
PROTEIN RICH

Fresh berries are an excellent source of vitamin C. Amazingly, 100g strawberries provides 98% of our daily needs, and in turn helps our bodies fight infectious agents. It is important to understand that while fruit such as berries do contain sugar it is not a source of sugar to be concerned by. The many health benefits of eating fresh fruit, especially berries, are well documented.

STRAWBERRIES ARE UNIQUE AS A FRUIT, WEARING THEIR TINY SEEDS ON THE OUTSIDE OF THE FRUIT RATHER THAN INSIDE.

BLUEBERRIES

are the perfect low kilojoule snack to tide you over between meals and are surprisingly satiating. A half-cup of berries has the same amount of fibre as a slice of wholegrain bread.

RASPBERRIES

share many of the super properties of other berries, such as antioxidant vitamins as well as valuable minerals such as potassium, magnesium and copper that collectively help control heart rate and blood pressure.

MULBERRIES

are not often available commercially however are worth seeking out for an array of health properties, uniquely for a berry, 100g contains 23% of the recommended daily intake of iron.

GOJI BERRIES CONTAIN LYCOPENE, A CAROTENOID ASSOCIATED WITH A REDUCED RISK OF CANCER, PARTICULARLY PROSTATE CANCER IN MEN. IN GENERAL THEIR HEALTH ATTRIBUTES ARE OVER-HYPED MAKING THEM RATHER EXPENSIVE, WHEN IN REALITY THEY ARE NUTRITIONALLY ON A PAR WITH BERRIES, RATHER THAN BEING SUPERIOR.

POMEGRANATES ARE FILLED WITH TIGHT CLUSTERS OF SOUR, YET SWEET SEEDS KNOWN AS ARILS. GOOD QUALITY POMEGRANATE JUICE IS MADE BY CRUSHING THE WHOLE FRUIT, SO THAT THE UNIQUE BLEND OF PHYTONUTRIENTS CONTAINED IN THE RIND ARE ALSO ACCESSED.

BERRIES

I AM

VITAMIN C

ANTIOXIDANTS

MINERALS

POMEGRANATES

go with... chocolate, ricotta, yoghurt, lamb, chicken, salads, grains and muesli.

THE *colour* OF OUR FOOD CAN TELL US LOTS OF THINGS. BERRIES HIGHLY HUED RED, BLUE AND PURPLE ARE INDICATIVE OF THEIR *high anthocyanins* CONTENT, AN ANTIOXIDANT THAT HAS BEEN SHOWN IN STUDIES TO AID CARDIOVASCULAR HEALTH.

I AM
LOW FAT
DAIRY FREE
EGG FREE

KEEP CHOPPED BANANAS IN A RESEALABLE PLASTIC BAG IN THE FREEZER TO MAKE EARLY MORNING BLENDING FASTER AND EASIER. YOU CAN REPLACE ALMOND MILK WITH ANY MILK YOU PREFER. TOP THE SORBET WITH ANY OF YOUR FAVOURITE FRUIT. SORBET CAN BE STORED IN THE FREEZER FOR UP TO 1 WEEK.

BANANA
BREAKFAST SORBET

4 MEDIUM FROZEN BANANAS (800G), BROKEN INTO PIECES

500G (1 POUND) FROZEN STRAWBERRIES

1 SMALL BEETROOT (BEETS) (100G), PEELED, CHOPPED COARSELY

1 TABLESPOON FINELY GRATED FRESH GINGER

2 CUPS (500ML) UNSWEETENED ALMOND MILK

250G (8 OUNCES) FRESH STRAWBERRIES, HALVED

2 MEDIUM GOLDEN KIWIFRUITS (170G), PEELED, SLICED THICKLY

1 TABLESPOON WHITE CHIA SEEDS

1 Working in two batches, place bananas, frozen strawberries, beetroot, ginger and almond milk in a blender; blend until smooth.

2 Pour mixture into a freezerproof container; cover with plastic wrap. Freeze for 6 hours or overnight until firm.

3 Working in two batches, scoop sorbet into blender; blend until smooth.

4 Pour sorbet into bowls; top with fresh strawberries, kiwifruit and chia seeds. Serve immediately.

prep time 15 minutes (+ freezing) **serves** 4
nutritional count per serving 15.8g total fat (1g saturated fat); 1466kJ (350 cal); 36.4g carbohydrate; 10.8g protein; 10.5g fibre

YOU CAN USE THE SAME WEIGHT OF OTHER FRUITS SUCH AS APRICOTS, APPLES, PEARS, BLUEBERRIES, BLACKBERRIES AND PLUMS. HAVE ALL YOUR DRY INGREDIENTS WEIGHED AND COMBINED THE NIGHT BEFORE, TO MAKE IT EASIER TO PREPARE THE NEXT MORNING.

FIG *And* RASPBERRY

BAKED PORRIDGE

1½ CUPS (135G) TRADITIONAL ROLLED OATS

1 TEASPOON GROUND GINGER

½ TEASPOON SEA SALT

2 TABLESPOONS COCONUT SUGAR

⅓ CUP (55G) DRY-ROASTED ALMONDS, CHOPPED COARSELY

3 CUPS (750ML) MILK

2 TABLESPOONS HONEY

2 TABLESPOONS OLIVE OIL

200G (6½ OUNCES) FRESH RASPBERRIES

8 FRESH FIGS (480G), TORN IN HALF

1 CUP (280G) GREEK-STYLE YOGHURT

1 Preheat oven to 180°C/350°F. Grease a 2 litre (8-cup) ovenproof dish.

2 Combine oats, ginger, salt, coconut sugar and half the almonds in a large bowl. Whisk milk, half the honey and the oil in a large jug until combined; add to oat mixture, stirring until just combined. Fold in half the raspberries and 5 of the figs. Spread mixture evenly into dish.

3 Bake porridge for 30 minutes or until oats are tender. Stand for 10 minutes. Top with remaining almonds, raspberries and figs; drizzle with remaining honey. Serve porridge with yoghurt.

prep + cook time 50 minutes **serves** 6

nutritional count per serving 20.6g total fat (6.3g saturated fat); 1880kJ (449 cal); 50.7g carbohydrate; 12.6g protein; 7.1g fibre

I AM
HIGH FIBRE
HIGH IN CALCIUM
EGG FREE

I AM
DAIRY FREE
GLUTEN FREE
LOW CARB

KIMCHI IS A TRADITIONAL KOREAN FERMENTED CABBAGE DISH FOUND IN ASIAN SUPERMARKETS. FREEZE REMAINING CANNED TOMATOES IN A RESEALABLE BAG FOR UP TO 3 MONTHS.

ONE·PAN EGGS
with KIMCHI

¼ CUP (60G) COCONUT OIL

1⅓ CUPS (300G) KIMCHI

½ X 400G (12½-OUNCE) CAN DICED TOMATOES

4 FREE-RANGE EGGS

½ CUP (40G) BEAN SPROUTS

¼ CUP LOOSELY PACKED FRESH CORIANDER (CILANTRO) LEAVES

¼ CUP LOOSELY PACKED FRESH MINT LEAVES

1 Heat coconut oil in a medium frying pan with a fitted lid over high heat. Add kimchi and tomatoes; cook, stirring, for 2 minutes or until combined and simmering. Season.

2 Using a wooden spoon, make four indents within the kimchi mixture. Carefully break an egg into each indent. Reduce heat to low; cook, covered, for 5 minutes or until egg whites are just set.

3 Serve immediately topped with sprouts and herbs.

prep + cook time 15 minutes **serves** 4

nutritional count per serving 19.7g total fat (15.4g saturated fat); 971kJ (232 cal); 4.1g carbohydrate; 8.6g protein; 2.2g fibre

serving suggestion Serve with char-grilled bread.

THIS RECIPE IS COELIAC AND PALEO FRIENDLY. MUESLI CAN BE STORED IN AN AIRTIGHT CONTAINER FOR UP TO 10 DAYS. DIVIDE MUESLI INTO INDIVIDUAL RESEALABLE BAGS FOR A HANDY SNACK. USE ORANGE RIND INSTEAD OF MANDARIN, IF YOU LIKE.

MANDARIN And CARDAMOM
NO-GRAIN MUESLI

2 MEDIUM MANDARINS (400G)

½ CUP (80G) ALMOND KERNELS, CHOPPED COARSELY

½ CUP (80G) SHELLED PISTACHIOS, CHOPPED COARSELY

½ CUP (60G) PECANS, CHOPPED COARSELY

¼ CUP (50G) PEPITAS (PUMPKIN SEED KERNELS)

½ CUP (60G) GROUND ALMONDS

1 TABLESPOON GROUND CARDAMOM

½ CUP (120G) COCONUT OIL, MELTED

2 TABLESPOONS HONEY

½ TEASPOON SEA SALT

2½ CUPS (125G) COCONUT FLAKES

1 Preheat oven to 160°C/325°F. Grease and line two large oven trays with baking paper.

2 Peel rind from mandarins. Using a small sharp knife, remove the white pith. Cut rind into thick strips. Combine mandarin rind with remaining ingredients except the coconut flakes in a large bowl. Using your hands, squeeze and rub the mixture together to release the oil from the mandarin rind; fold in coconut flakes. Spread mixture evenly between trays.

3 Bake muesli for 20 minutes, stirring occasionally into clumps, or until lightly golden. Cool on trays for 15 minutes to crisp slightly.

4 Serve muesli with milk or yoghurt and fresh fruit such as mandarin and blood orange.

prep + cook time 30 minutes (+ cooling)

serves 4 (makes 5 cups)

nutritional count per serving 84.5g total fat (39g saturated fat); 4052kJ (968 cal); 32g carbohydrate; 16.9g protein; 8.5g fibre

I AM

HIGH PROTEIN

VITAMIN RICH

VEGETARIAN

YOU CAN ALSO USE SILVER BEET (SWISS CHARD),
KALE OR SPINACH INSTEAD OF RAINBOW SWISS CHARD.
RECIPE IS BEST MADE JUST BEFORE SERVING.

RAINBOW CHARD *And* GARLIC BAKED EGGS

6 MEDIUM RAINBOW CHARD LEAVES WITH STEMS (330G)

2 TABLESPOONS OLIVE OIL

2 CLOVES GARLIC, CRUSHED

8 FREE-RANGE EGGS

⅓ CUP (80ML) CREAM

2 TABLESPOONS ROASTED SKINLESS HAZELNUTS, CHOPPED COARSELY

2 TABLESPOONS SMALL FRESH FLAT-LEAF PARSLEY LEAVES

BULLS BLOOD LEAVES, TO SERVE

1 Preheat oven to 180°C/350°F. Grease four 1 cup (250ml) shallow ovenproof dishes.

2 Chop chard stems into 5cm (2-inch) lengths; coarsely chop leaves.

3 Heat oil in a large frying pan over medium heat; cook chard stems, stirring for 2 minutes or until just tender. Add garlic and chard leaves; cook, stirring for 2 minutes or until garlic is fragrant and leaves have wilted. Season.

4 Divide chard mixture into dishes. Carefully break two eggs into each dish, then add cream.

5 Bake for 15 minutes or until eggs are just set. Serve topped with hazelnuts, parsley and bulls blood leaves.

prep + cook time 30 minutes **serves** 4
nutritional count per serving 29.3g total fat (9.4g saturated fat); 1417kJ (338 cal); 2g carbohydrate; 16g protein; 2.6g fibre
serving suggestion Serve with char-grilled bread.

TROPICAL JUICE

prep time 10 minutes **serves** 2 (makes 2 cups)

Place 150g (4½oz) papaya, 150g (4½oz) peeled fresh pineapple, 80g (2½oz) frozen mango, ½ cup coconut water, ½ cup pomegranate juice and ice-cubes in a high-powdered juice blender; blend until smooth. Pour into glasses; top with 1 tablespoon toasted shaved coconut and 1 teaspoon pomegranate seeds.

ICED CHAI TEA

prep time 20 minutes (+ refrigeration)
serves 2 (makes 2 cups)

Place 1 chai tea bag in a heatproof jug and add ¾ cup boiling water. Stand for 10 minutes to infuse. Remove and discard tea bag. Add ¾ cup chilled water; refrigerate until cold. Place chai tea in a high-powered juice blender with ½ cup coconut milk, 1½ tablespoons finely grated palm sugar and ice-cubes; blend until smooth. Pour into glasses; sprinkle with cocoa powder.

GREEN TEA & APPLE

prep time 20 minutes (+ refrigeration)

serves 2 (makes 2 cups)

Place 1 green tea bag in a heatproof jug and add ¾ cup boiling water. Stand for 10 minutes to infuse. Remove and discard tea bag. Add ¾ cup chilled water; refrigerate until cold. Place iced tea in a high-powdered juice blender with 1 peeled, cored, green-skinned apple, ¼ teaspoon finely grated fresh ginger, 2 tablespoons honey and 2 tablespoons fresh mint leaves; blend until smooth. Pour into glasses; top with ice-cubes.

BREAKFAST SMOOTHIE

prep time 10 minutes **serves** 2 (makes 2 cups)

Place ½ cup greek-style yoghurt, 75g (2½oz) frozen mixed berries, 1 tablespoon honey, 2 teaspoons ground flaxseed, 1 cup milk in a high-powdered juice blender; blend until smooth. Pour into glasses; top with 42g (1½oz) crumbled, crunchy muesli bar.

YOU CAN MAKE THIS THE NIGHT BEFORE UP TO THE END
OF STEP 1. REHEAT WITH MILK OR SERVE COLD THE NEXT DAY.
COOL ANY LEFTOVER PORRIDGE AND KEEP, COVERED, IN THE FRIDGE
FOR UP TO 3 DAYS. STIR IN A LITTLE EXTRA MILK TO SERVE.

THREE-GRAIN
MAPLE SYRUP PORRIDGE

1 CUP (160G) BROWN RICE

½ CUP (100G) PEARL BARLEY

½ CUP (45G) STEEL CUT OATS

1.25 LITRES (5 CUPS) WATER

1 CINNAMON STICK, HALVED

½ VANILLA BEAN, SEEDS SCRAPED

½ TEASPOON SALT

½ CUP (125ML) MILK

2 TABLESPOONS PURE MAPLE SYRUP

1 RIPE PERSIMMON (120G), SLICED THINLY

125G (4 OUNCES) BLUEBERRIES

¼ CUP (60G) POMEGRANATE SEEDS

¼ CUP (35G) HAZELNUTS, TOASTED,
CHOPPED COARSELY

¾ CUP (200G) VANILLA YOGHURT

2 TABLESPOONS PURE MAPLE SYRUP, EXTRA

PINCH OF GROUND CINNAMON

1 Combine rice, barley, oats, the water, cinnamon stick, vanilla bean and seeds and salt in a medium saucepan over high heat; bring to the boil. Reduce heat to low; simmer, covered, for 40 minutes, stirring occasionally to prevent sticking to base of pan, or until grains are tender with a slight bite.

2 Stir in milk and maple syrup; cook, stirring for 5 minutes or until heated through.

3 Serve porridge topped with persimmon, blueberries, pomegranate seeds, hazelnuts and yoghurt; drizzle with extra maple syrup and sprinkle with ground cinnamon.

prep + cook time 50 minutes **serves** 4
nutritional count per serving 10.9g total fat (2.5g saturated fat); 2136kJ (510 cal); 87g carbohydrate; 11.8g protein; 8.4g fibre

WE USED A NUT, FRUIT AND SEED MIX CONSISTING OF ALMONDS, CASHEWS, SULTANAS, CHOPPED DRIED APRICOTS, PEPITAS AND SUNFLOWER SEEDS. YOU CAN USE ANY COMBINATION OF NUTS, DRIED FRUIT AND SEEDS YOU PREFER.

FRUIT *And* NUT MUFFINS

¾ CUP (120G) WHOLEMEAL SELF-RAISING FLOUR

½ CUP (75G) WHITE SELF-RAISING FLOUR

¾ CUP (120G) NUT, FRUIT AND SEED MIX, CHOPPED COARSELY

½ CUP (140G) VANILLA YOGHURT

½ CUP (125ML) MILK

¼ CUP (90G) HONEY

1 FREE-RANGE EGG

¼ CUP (60ML) OLIVE OIL

1 SMALL PEAR (180G), CHOPPED FINELY

⅔ CUP (110G) NUT, FRUIT AND SEED MIX, EXTRA, CHOPPED COARSELY

2 TABLESPOONS HONEY, EXTRA

1 Preheat oven to 180°C/350°F. Line a 12-hole (⅓ cup/80ml) muffin pan with paper cases.

2 Combine flours and nut mix in a large bowl. Whisk yoghurt, milk, honey, egg and oil in a jug; pour into flour mixture, stir until just combined. Fold in the pear.

3 Spoon mixture into paper cases; sprinkle with extra nut mix.

4 Bake muffins for 18 minutes or until a skewer inserted in the centre comes out clean. Serve warm muffins drizzled with extra honey

prep + cook time 40 minutes **makes** 12

nutritional count per muffin 10.7g total fat (1.9g saturated fat); 960kJ (229 cal); 27g carbohydrate; 5.6g protein; 2.8g fibre

BANANA DATE LOAF
with HONEY SPICED LABNE

You will need to start this recipe a day ahead. Muslin is available from fabric or craft stores. You will need 1¼ ripe bananas.

½ CUP (55G) COARSELY CHOPPED WALNUTS

½ CUP (45G) TRADITIONAL ROLLED OATS

1 TABLESPOON COCONUT OIL

1 TABLESPOON PURE MAPLE SYRUP

1 CUP (300G) MASHED RIPE BANANA

2 TEASPOONS VANILLA EXTRACT

¾ CUP (180ML) BUTTERMILK

200G (6½ OUNCES) MEDJOOL DATES, PITTED, CHOPPED COARSELY

2 CUPS (300G) HIGH-FIBRE SELF-RAISING FLOUR

1 TEASPOON BICARBONATE OF SODA (BAKING SODA)

1½ TEASPOONS BAKING POWDER

⅓ CUP (80G) COCONUT OIL, EXTRA

HONEY SPICED LABNE

500G (1 POUND) GREEK-STYLE YOGHURT

2 TABLESPOONS HONEY

2 TEASPOONS GROUND CARDAMOM

1 Make honey spiced labne.

2 Preheat oven to 180°C/350°F. Grease and line a 10cm x 20cm (4-inch x 8-inch) loaf pan with baking paper.

3 Combine walnuts, oats, coconut oil and maple syrup in a bowl. Place half the walnut mixture on a baking-paper-lined oven tray. Bake 10 minutes or until golden; cool.

4 Place banana, extract, reserved labne liquid, buttermilk and half the dates in a blender; blend until smooth.

5 Sift flour, soda and baking powder into a large bowl. Add banana mixture, remaining dates, extra coconut oil and roasted walnut mixture; stir to combine. Spoon mixture into pan, smooth surface. Sprinkle with remaining walnut mixture.

6 Bake for 1 hour 10 minutes or until a skewer inserted in the centre comes out clean. Leave in pan 15 minutes; turn, top-side up, onto a wire rack to cool completely.

7 Serve bread with honey spiced labne.

honey spiced labne Line a sieve with muslin; place over a medium bowl. Spoon yoghurt into sieve, gather cloth and tie into a ball with kitchen string. Refrigerate for 24 hours, gently squeezing occasionally to encourage the liquid to drain. Reserve ½ cup of draining liquid to add in step 4. Place labne in a medium bowl with honey and cardamom; mix well. Refrigerate until required.

prep + cook time 1 hour 40 minutes (+ refrigeration)
serves 8
nutritional count per serving 22.3g total fat (14.8g saturated fat); 2070kJ (494 cal); 60.6g carbohydrate; 10g protein; 6.8g fibre

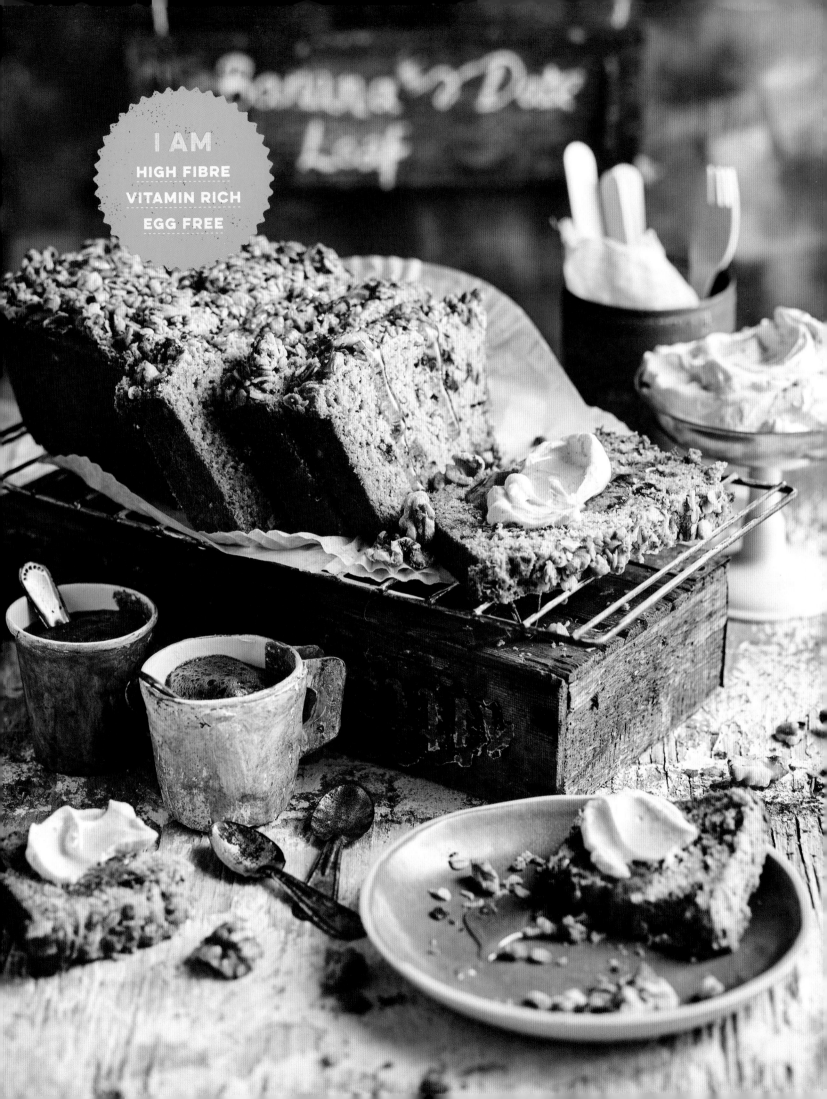

I AM
HIGH FIBRE
VITAMIN RICH
EGG FREE

NO-KNEAD FENNEL And BEETROOT SPELT BREAD

You will need to start this recipe a day ahead. We used a cast iron saucepan, but any heavy-based pan can be used. For a sweet variation, add nuts, dried fruit and honey.

1 MEDIUM BEETROOT (BEETS) (150G), PEELED, GRATED COARSELY

3 TEASPOONS FENNEL SEEDS

3 CUPS (450G) SPELT FLOUR

1 TEASPOON TABLE SALT

1 TEASPOON DRIED YEAST

1 TABLESPOON OLIVE OIL

1¼ CUPS (310ML) WARM WATER

1 TEASPOON SALT FLAKES

1 Spread beetroot onto paper towel; stand for 1 hour to dry.

2 Place 2 teaspoons of the fennel seeds in a small frying pan; cook, stirring for 30 seconds or until fragrant.

3 Combine flour, table salt, toasted fennel seeds, yeast, oil, the water and beetroot in a large bowl. Cover with plastic wrap and a tea towel; stand to slowly rise for 14 hours.

4 Place a 24cm (9½-inch) (base measurement) cast iron casserole dish with a firm fitting lid in the oven; preheat to 240°C/475°F. (The dish needs to be as hot as the oven before you put the dough inside.)

5 Turn dough onto a floured surface; shape into a large ball. Divide dough into eight portions; shape each portion into a roll. Arrange rolls, side-by-side, in a circle, on a large sheet of baking paper. Sprinkle with salt flakes and remaining fennel seeds. Cover; stand for 1 hour.

6 Transfer rolls on paper into the hot dish; cover with lid. Bake for 20 minutes; remove lid. Bake for a further 12 minutes or until bread sounds hollow when tapped. Transfer bread to a wire rack. Serve warm or cool.

prep + cook time 50 minutes (+ standing) **makes** 8 rolls
nutritional count per roll 3.1g total fat (0.4g saturated fat); 985kJ (235 cal); 42g carbohydrate; 7.7g protein; 2.7g fibre
serving suggestion Serve with ricotta and honey.

KUMARA ROSTI

WITH ROASTED VEGETABLES

170G (5½ OUNCES) ASPARAGUS, TRIMMED

1 MEDIUM RED CAPSICUM (BELL PEPPER) (200G), CUT INTO 1CM (½-INCH) STRIPS

2 TABLESPOONS OLIVE OIL

750G (1½ POUNDS) KUMARA (ORANGE SWEET POTATO), PEELED, GRATED COARSELY

1 MEDIUM RED ONION (170G), SLICED THINLY

2 TABLESPOONS RICE FLOUR

1 TABLESPOON FRESH THYME LEAVES

1 MEDIUM AVOCADO (250G), CHOOPED

100G (3 OUNCES) MARINATED GOAT'S FETTA IN OLIVE OIL, RESERVE 1 TABLESPOON OF THE OIL

KALE SPROUTS, TO SERVE

1 Preheat a flat-based sandwich press on high. Toss asparagus and capsicum in half the olive oil; season. Place in sandwich press, close; cook for 5 minutes or until lightly grilled. Cut asparagus in half lengthways.

2 Meanwhile, squeeze out excess moisture from kumara. Combine kumara, onion, flour, thyme and remaining olive oil in a medium bowl; season.

3 Spoon ⅓ cup measures of kumara mixture, in two batches, on base plate of sandwich press. Close press to flatten; cook for 7 minutes or until crisp and golden.

4 Serve rösti topped with asparagus, capsicum, avocado and crumbled fetta. Drizzle with reserved marinating oil and top with kale sprouts.

prep + cook time 30 minutes **serves** 4
nutritional count per serving 23.9g total fat (7.3g saturated fat); 1855kJ (443 cal); 42g carbohydrate; 11.6g protein; 7.7g fibre
tip Rösti and vegetables can also be cooked in a non-stick frying pan.

I AM
NUT FREE
GLUTEN FREE
LOW GI

SUPER LUNCHES

NO LONGER JUST ABOUT SANDWICHES, IF IT'S TRANSPORTABLE IT'S SUITABLE. SOUPS AND SALADS, VEGIE WRAPS AND INDIVIDUAL TARTS, CAN ALL BE PREPARED AHEAD AND PACKAGED UP FOR WORK THE NEXT DAY.

FREEKEH IS ROASTED GREENWHEAT. IT HAS A DELICIOUS NUTTY TASTE AND TEXTURE AND IS AVAILABLE FROM THE HEALTH FOOD SECTION IN MAJOR SUPERMARKETS AND HEALTH FOOD STORES.

FREEKEH TABBOULEH
with BEETROOT

½ CUP (100G) CRACKED GREENWHEAT FREEKEH

250G (8 OUNCES) BABY ROMA (EGG) TOMATOES, HALVED

1 SMALL RED ONION (100G), SLICED THINLY

1 LARGE BEETROOT (BEETS) (200G), PEELED, CUT INTO THIN MATCHSTICKS

½ CUP (50G) WALNUTS, ROASTED, CHOPPED

1 CUP FRESH FLAT-LEAF PARSLEY LEAVES

½ CUP FRESH SMALL MINT LEAVES

LEMON YOGHURT DRESSING

½ CUP (140G) GREEK-STYLE YOGHURT

½ TEASPOON FINELY GRATED LEMON RIND

1 TABLESPOON LEMON JUICE

1 Place freekeh in a medium saucepan of water; bring to the boil. Reduce heat to low; simmer, partially covered, for 20 minutes until tender. Drain. Rinse under cold water; drain well.

2 Meanwhile, make lemon yoghurt dressing.

3 Place freekeh in a large bowl with tomatoes, onion, beetroot, walnuts and herbs; toss gently to combine. Drizzle with dressing. If you like, sprinkle with extra strips of lemon rind (see tips).

lemon yoghurt dressing Combine ingredients in a small bowl; season to taste.

prep + cook time 35 minutes **serves** 4

nutritional count per serving 11.7g total fat (2.6g saturated fat); 1136kJ (271 cal); 29.8g carbohydrate; 9.4g protein; 10g fibre

tips Use a julienne peeler to easily cut the beetroot into matchsticks. If you have one, use a zester to create strips of lemon rind. If you don't have one, use a vegetable peeler to remove the rind, avoiding the white pith, then cut it into long thin strips.

I AM
HIGH FIBRE
PROTEIN RICH
LOW GI

I AM

PROTEIN RICH

HIGH IN OMEGA 3

DAIRY FREE

UNCOOKED RISSOLES CAN BE MADE A DAY AHEAD; STORE COVERED, IN THE FRIDGE. UNCOOKED PATTIES CAN ALSO BE FROZEN FOR UP TO 3 MONTHS. THAW IN THE FRIDGE OVERNIGHT.

KUMARA TUNA RISSOLES
WITH SPICY HUMMUS

560G (1 POUND) KUMARA (ORANGE SWEET POTATO), PEELED, CUT INTO 1.5CM (¾-INCH) PIECES

1 GREEN ONION (SCALLION), SLICED THINLY

¼ CUP COARSELY CHOPPED FRESH CORIANDER (CILANTRO) LEAVES

2 TABLESPOONS PEPITAS (PUMPKIN SEEDS)

125G (4 OUNCES) CANNED TUNA IN SPRINGWATER, DRAINED

1½ TABLESPOONS OLIVE OIL

4 X 50G (1½-OUNCE) PITTA BREAD, TOASTED

50G (1½ OUNCES) BABY SPINACH LEAVES

LEMON CHEEKS, TO SERVE

SPICY HUMMUS

400G (12½ OUNCES) CANNED CHICKPEAS (GARBANZO BEANS), DRAINED, RINSED

1 CLOVE GARLIC, CRUSHED

½ TEASPOON DRIED CHILLI FLAKES

2 TEASPOONS GROUND CUMIN

1 TABLESPOON LEMON JUICE

1½ TABLESPOONS OLIVE OIL

¼ CUP (60ML) WATER

1 Place kumara in a medium microwave-safe bowl; cover. Microwave on HIGH (100%) for 6 minutes, stirring, every 2 minutes, or until very tender. Add green onion, coriander and pepitas, season; mix well, mashing some of the kumara to combine. Flake through the tuna; stir until just combined.

2 Shape ¼-cups of kumara mixture into 8 rissoles; place on an oven tray. Refrigerate 20 minutes.

3 Meanwhile, make spicy hummus.

4 Heat oil in a large non-stick frying pan over medium heat; cook rissoles, in batches, for 4 minutes each side or until golden brown.

5 Serve rissoles with hummus, pitta bread, spinach leaves and lemon cheeks.

spicy hummus Process chickpeas, garlic, chilli flakes, cumin, juice and oil in a food processor until smooth. With the motor operating, gradually add the water; process until combined. Season. Serve sprinkled with a little more cumin.

prep + cook time 40 minutes (+ refrigeration) serves 4
nutritional count per serving 20g total fat (3.3g saturated fat); 2155kJ (515 cal); 59g carbohydrate; 21.2g protein; 8.2g fibre

SOUP CAN BE MADE UP TO 3 DAYS AHEAD; KEEP, COVERED, IN THE FRIDGE. REFRIGERATE GINGER MIXTURE IN A SEPARATE CONTAINER. SOUP CAN BE FROZEN FOR UP TO 3 MONTHS.

GREEN 'SMOOTHIE'

½ CUP (125ML) EXTRA VIRGIN OLIVE OIL

1 MEDIUM LEEK (350G), WHITE PART ONLY, CHOPPED FINELY

1 CLOVE GARLIC, CRUSHED

2 TEASPOONS FINELY GRATED FRESH GINGER

150G (4½ OUNCES) BROCCOLI, CHOPPED

1 SMALL PEAR (180G), CHOPPED COARSELY

2 TABLESPOONS GROUND ALMONDS

1 LITRE (4 CUPS) SALT-REDUCED CHICKEN STOCK

80G (2½ OUNCES) BABY SPINACH LEAVES

5CM (2-INCH) PIECE FRESH GINGER (25G), EXTRA, PEELED, CUT INTO THIN MATCHSTICKS

¼ CUP (20G) NATURAL FLAKED ALMONDS

1 Heat 2 tablespoons of the oil in a large saucepan over low heat; cook leek, garlic and grated ginger, stirring, for 8 minutes or until leek is soft. Increase heat to medium, add broccoli, pear and ground almonds; cook, stirring, for 2 minutes or until broccoli and pear are hot and vegetables are coated in almonds.

2 Add stock; bring to the boil. Reduce heat; simmer, covered, for 10 minutes or until broccoli is tender. Stir in spinach; stand for 10 minutes.

3 Blend or process soup, in batches, until smooth. Return soup to pan; stir over heat until hot. Season.

4 Meanwhile, heat remaining oil in a medium frying pan over high heat; cook extra ginger, stirring occasionally, for 1 minute or until golden. Drain on paper towel; season. Add flaked almonds to same pan; cook, stirring, for 30 seconds or until browned lightly. Drain on paper towel.

5 Ladle soup into serving bowls, top with toasted flaked almonds and crisp ginger.

prep + cook time 40 minutes **serves** 4
nutritional count per serving 35g total fat (5.2g saturated fat); 1615kJ (386 cal); 10.3g carbohydrate; 6.2g protein; 6g fibre

I AM

DAIRY FREE

VITAMIN RICH

LOW CARB

I AM
EGG FREE
PROTEIN RICH
LOW GI

ZUCCHINI *And* FREEKEH
CHICKEN SOUP

½ CUP (100G) CRACKED GREENWHEAT FREEKEH

1 TABLESPOON OLIVE OIL

1 MEDIUM LEEK (350G), WHITE PART ONLY, HALVED, SLICED THINLY

4 CLOVES GARLIC, SLICED THINLY

1.25 LITRES (5 CUPS) WATER

4 CHICKEN THIGH CUTLETS (800G), TRIMMED

150G (4½ OUNCES) GREEN BEANS, TRIMMED, CUT INTO 2CM (¾-INCH) LENGTHS

1 LARGE ZUCCHINI (150G), SLICED THINLY

½ CUP (60G) FROZEN PEAS

2 TABLESPOONS CHOPPED FRESH FLAT-LEAF PARSLEY

1 Place freekeh in a medium saucepan of water; bring to the boil. Reduce heat to low; simmer, partially covered, for 15 minutes until almost tender. Drain.

2 Meanwhile, heat oil a large saucepan over medium heat; cook leek, stirring, for 4 minutes until softened. Add garlic; cook, stirring, for 2 minutes.

3 Add the water and chicken; bring to the boil. Reduce heat to low; cook, covered, for 30 minutes or until chicken is cooked. Remove chicken from stock, discard skin and bones; shred meat. Return shredded chicken to pan with beans and freekeh, then season; cook, uncovered, for 5 minutes. Add zucchini and peas; cook for 3 minutes until tender.

4 Ladle soup into bowls; serve topped with parsley.

prep + cook time 1 hour **serves** 4 (makes 8 cups)
nutritional count per serving 25.7g total fat (8g saturated fat); 1865kJ (445 cal); 22.3g carbohydrate; 29.7g protein; 9g fibre
tip For a more intense flavour, use homemade chicken stock instead of water.

Red or green cabbage? ONE CUP OF EITHER TYPE WILL PROVIDE YOU WITH EIGHT TYPES OF VITAMINS AND MINERALS. THE NOTABLE DIFFERENCE BETWEEN THE TWO IS IN VITAMIN A CONTENT, WITH RED CABBAGE CONTAINING 10 TIMES THAT OF GREEN. VITAMIN A IS NEEDED TO KEEP THE SKIN AND IMMUNE SYSTEM HEALTHY. ON THE OTHER HAND, GREEN CABBAGE HAS DOUBLE THE AMOUNT OF VITAMIN K, AN IMPORTANT VITAMIN FOR BONE MINERALISATION.

SILVER BEET young leaves can be shredded and added to salads. Both the leaf and most of the white stem can be wilted in olive oil; cook stems first before adding the quicker cooking leaf.

KALE different types abound: purple to green, to young and more mature. Small leaves are better for salads. To prepare kale, strip away the leaf, then discard the tougher central stems.

CAVOLO NERO is also known as Tuscan cabbage. To prepare this winter green, trim off the long stems at the base of the leaves. Wilt in olive oil with garlic and finish with a squeeze of lemon juice.

RAINBOW CHARD a hybrid of silver beet and beetroot, its stems are brightly hued yellow, pink, red and purple. Nutritionally it is near identical to silver beet, packed with minerals, iron and the vitamins E, A, B6 and K.

Brussels sprouts

Its past unpopularity comes from not knowing how to cook it properly – over cooking produces a sulphurus odour, derived from thiocyanates, one of several powerful flavonoids it possesses. It also contains large amounts of vitamin K, a vitamin thought to prevent or at least delay the onset of Alzheimer's disease.

THREE THINGS TO DO *with* BRUSSELS SPROUTS....

RAW *and* SHAVED
In a salad for a coleslaw twist.

STIR-FRIED
With your favourite asian sauce.

ROASTED
With garlic, olive oil, ground cumin and a little honey.

Broccoli CONTAINS A COMPOUND THAT, DEPENDING ON YOUR UNIQUE SET OF TASTE BUDS, WILL TASTE BITTER TO SOME INDIVIDUALS AND TASTELESS TO OTHERS.

SPIRULINA (POWDER) CONTAINS MORE THAN 100 NUTRIENTS.

GREENS

EAT
YOUR
GREENS

BRASSICA IS THE NAME GIVEN TO A BROAD FAMILY OF VEGETABLES THAT ARE IMPORTANT FOR THEIR *soluble fibre*, POTENT *anticancer properties* AND HIGH LEVELS OF *vitamins*. THESE VERSATILE VEGETABLES RANGE IN TASTE FROM SWEET TO MUSTARDY OR PEPPERY.

COVER HANDLE OF FRYING PAN WITH SEVERAL LAYERS OF FOIL TO PREVENT SCORCHING UNDER THE GRILL. TORTILLA CAN BE MADE A DAY AHEAD, STORE, COVERED IN THE FRIDGE.

KUMARA TORTILLA
with RICOTTA HARISSA

2 TABLESPOONS OLIVE OIL

1 MEDIUM WHITE ONION (150G), SLICED THINLY

300G (9½ OUNCES) KUMARA (ORANGE SWEET POTATO), PEELED, SLICED VERY THINLY

12 FREE-RANGE EGGS, BEATEN LIGHTLY

250G (8 OUNCES) FRESH RICOTTA

1 TABLESPOON HARISSA PASTE

1 TABLESPOON SUNFLOWER SEEDS

2 TABLESPOONS COARSELY CHOPPED ALMONDS

¼ CUP FRESH CORIANDER (CILANTRO) LEAVES

1 TABLESPOON OLIVE OIL, EXTRA

1 Heat half the oil in a 20cm x 25cm (8-inch x 10-inch) (base measurement) ovenproof frying pan over medium heat. Add onion and kumara; carefully stir to coat in oil; season. Reduce heat to low; cover, cook for 20 minutes or until tender.

2 Preheat a grill (broiler) to high.

3 Transfer kumara mixture to a large bowl. Add egg; stir well to coat. Heat remaining oil in same pan over medium heat. Add egg mixture; reduce heat to very low. Cook for 10 minutes or until partially set. Place under grill; cook for 5 minutes or until golden and cooked through. Stand for 5 minutes.

4 Serve tortilla topped with ricotta, harissa, sunflower seeds, almonds and coriander; drizzle with extra oil.

prep + cook time 45 minutes (+ cooling) **serves** 4
nutritional count per serving 34.4g total fat (10.4g saturated fat); 1982kJ (473 cal); 12.9g carbohydrate; 27.8g protein; 2.2g fibre

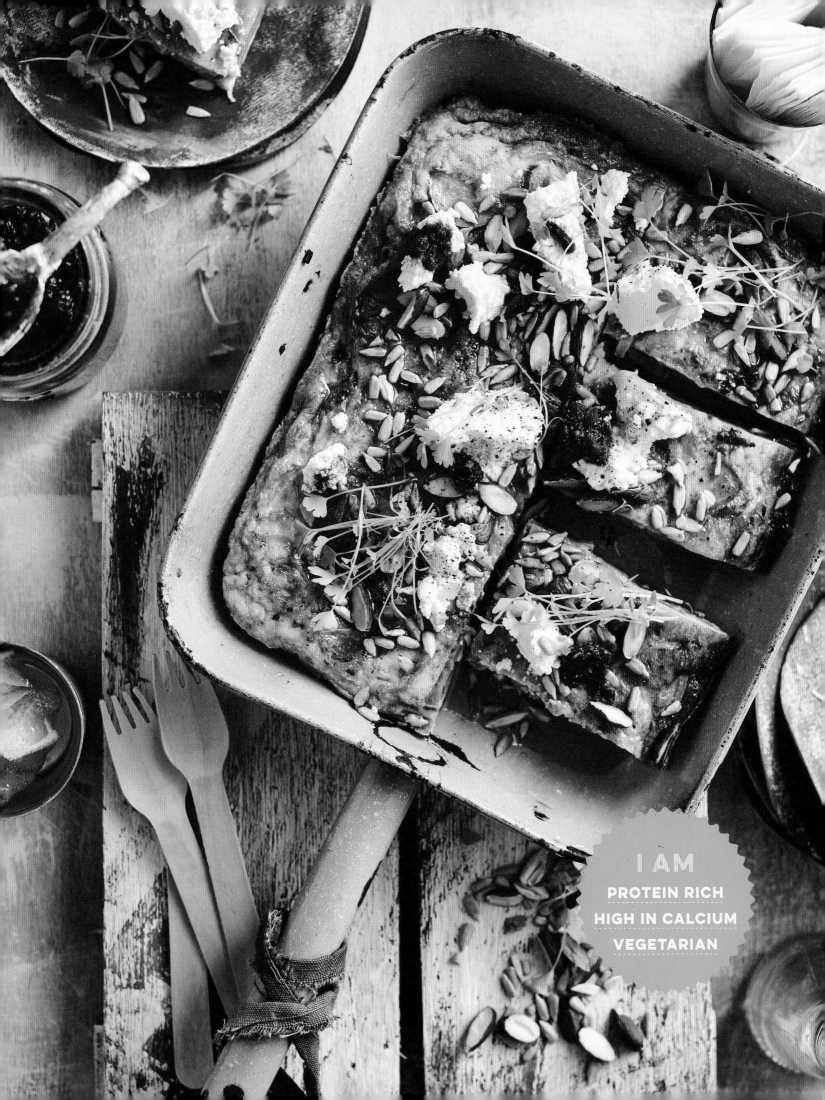

I AM
PROTEIN RICH
HIGH IN CALCIUM
VEGETARIAN

I AM
EGG FREE
PROTEIN RICH
LOW FAT

USE A VEGETABLE PEELER TO PEEL CUCUMBER INTO LONG THIN RIBBONS. DRESSING CAN BE MADE 2 DAYS AHEAD; KEEP REFRIGERATED. THE WASABI PEA CRUMBS ALSO WORK WELL AS A COATING FOR FIRM WHITE FISH AS FISH FINGERS.

WASABI CHICKEN
And EDAMAME SALAD

100G (3 OUNCES) WASABI PEAS

½ CUP (125ML) MILK

8 CHICKEN TENDERLOINS (600G), SLICED LENGTHWAYS

⅔ CUP (160G) FROZEN SHELLED EDAMAME (SOY BEANS), THAWED

60G (2 OUNCES) BABY SPINACH LEAVES

60G (2 OUNCES) RED VEIN SORREL

1 MEDIUM LEBANESE CUCUMBER (130G), CUT INTO RIBBONS

1 MEDIUM AVOCADO (250G), SLICED

1 TABLESPOON DRAINED PICKLED GINGER, CHOPPED COARSELY

1 SHEET NORI, CRUMBLED COARSELY

JAPANESE DRESSING

1 TABLESPOON RICE WINE VINEGAR

2 TEASPOONS SESAME SEEDS, TOASTED

2 TABLESPOONS MIRIN

2 TEASPOONS TAMARI

½ TEASPOON WASABI PASTE

1 SMALL CLOVE GARLIC, CRUSHED

1 Preheat oven to 180°C/350°F. Line two oven trays with baking paper.

2 Make japanese dressing.

3 Pulse wasabi peas in a food processor until finely chopped; transfer to a medium shallow dish. Place milk in another medium shallow dish.

4 Season chicken. Dip chicken in milk then coat in wasabi peas. Place chicken 5cm (2 inches) apart on trays. Bake for 15 minutes or until cooked through.

5 Meanwhile, boil, steam or microwave edamame until tender; drain. Refresh in a bowl of iced water; drain. Place edamame in a large bowl with spinach, sorrel, cucumber, avocado, ginger and nori.

6 Thickly slice chicken, gently fold through salad; drizzle with dressing. Serve immediately.

japanese dressing Place ingredients in a screw-top jar; shake well. Season to taste.

prep + cook time 40 minutes **serves** 4

nutritional count per serving 16.9g total fat (3.9g saturated fat); 1917kJ (458 cal); 26.4g carbohydrate; 46g protein; 2.7g fibre

SMOKED TUNA
BROCCOLINI *And* QUINOA SALAD

½ CUP (100G) RED QUINOA, RINSED

1 LITRE (4 CUPS) WATER

1 RED SHALLOT (25G), SLICED THINLY

1 SMALL RED CAPSICUM (BELL PEPPER) (150G)

1 SMALL YELLOW CAPSICUM (BELL PEPPER) (150G)

OLIVE OIL COOKING SPRAY

350G (11 OUNCES) BROCCOLINI

2 X 125G (4-OUNCE) CANS SMOKED TUNA IN OLIVE OIL, DRAINED

½ CUP (50G) WALNUTS, ROASTED

⅓ CUP FRESH FLAT-LEAF PARSLEY LEAVES

DRESSING

⅓ CUP (80ML) OLIVE OIL

¼ CUP (60ML) LEMON JUICE

1 CLOVE GARLIC, CRUSHED

1 Place quinoa and the water in a medium saucepan; bring to the boil. Reduce heat to low; cook, covered, for 12 minutes or until tender. Drain.

2 Meanwhile, make dressing.

3 Place quinoa in a medium bowl with shallot and half the dressing; toss to combine.

4 Quarter capsicums; discard seeds and membranes. Cut each piece of capsicum in half lengthways. Spray capsicum and broccolini with oil; cook, on a heated oiled grill plate (or grill or barbecue) over medium-high heat for 5 minutes each side or until cooked through.

5 Serve quinoa mixture topped with capsicum, broccolini, tuna, walnuts and parsley; drizzle with remaining dressing.

dressing Place ingredients in a screw-top jar; shake well.

prep + cook time 40 minutes **serves** 4

nutritional count per serving 37.5g total fat (4.8g saturated fat); 2215kJ (529 cal); 21.6g carbohydrate; 25.3g protein; 7.6g fibre

tip Use a lemon-infused olive oil for added flavour and richness.

I AM
HIGH FIBRE
PROTEIN RICH
EGG FREE

I AM
HIGH FIBRE
PROTEIN RICH
LOW FAT

HEARTY LENTIL
And VEGETABLE SOUP

1 TABLESPOON OLIVE OIL

1 MEDIUM BROWN ONION (150G), CHOPPED FINELY

3 CLOVES GARLIC, CRUSHED

2 TEASPOONS FINELY GRATED FRESH GINGER

1 TEASPOON CUMIN SEEDS, CRUSHED COARSELY

1 FRESH LONG RED CHILLI, CHOPPED FINELY

1 MEDIUM CARROT (120G), CHOPPED FINELY

2 TRIMMED CELERY STALKS (200G), CHOPPED FINELY

2 FRESH BAY LEAVES

3 FRESH THYME SPRIGS

1¼ CUPS (185G) DRIED FRENCH-STYLE GREEN LENTILS, RINSED

¼ CUP (70G) TOMATO PASTE

1.5 LITRES (6 CUPS) SALT-REDUCED CHICKEN STOCK

1½ TABLESPOONS LEMON JUICE

⅓ CUP (25G) SHAVED PARMESAN

1 FRESH SMALL RED CHILLI, EXTRA, SLICED THINLY

1 Heat oil in a large saucepan over medium-high heat; cook onion, garlic, ginger, cumin, chilli, carrot and celery, stirring, for 10 minutes or until softened.

2 Add bay leaves, thyme, lentils, tomato paste and stock; bring to the boil. Reduce heat; simmer, uncovered, for 20 minutes or until lentils are tender. Stir in juice; season to taste.

3 Ladle soup into bowls; serve topped with parmesan and extra chilli.

prep + cook time 50 minutes serves 4

nutritional count per serving 9.6g total fat (2.7g saturated fat); 1182kJ (282 cal); 27.5g carbohydrate; 17.5g protein; 10.7g fibre

tip For a vegetarian option use vegetable stock instead of chicken stock.

CUT THE VEGETABLES THE SAME SIZE. WRAPS CAN BE MADE THE NIGHT BEFORE, PLACED IN A LUNCH BOX LINED WITH BAKING PAPER, READY FOR THE NEXT DAY.

TOFU *And* MIXED VEGETABLE
WOMBOK WRAPS

2 TABLESPOONS HOISIN SAUCE

1 TEASPOON SESAME OIL

400G (12½ OUNCES) SILKEN FIRM TOFU, SLICED, CUT INTO 1CM (½-INCH) PIECES

1 SMALL CARROT (70G), CUT INTO THIN MATCHSTICKS

1 LEBANESE CUCUMBER (130G), SEEDS REMOVED, CUT INTO THIN MATCHSTICKS

⅓ CUP (80ML) WHITE VINEGAR

190G (6 OUNCES) BROCCOLINI

8 LARGE WOMBOK (NAPA CABBAGE) LEAVES (600G)

4 GREEN ONIONS (SCALLIONS), SLICED FINELY

1 CUP FRESH CORIANDER (CILANTRO) LEAVES

1 CUP FRESH VIETNAMESE MINT OR MINT LEAVES

1 TABLESPOON RICE MALT SYRUP

2 TEASPOONS FISH SAUCE

1 FRESH LONG RED CHILLI, SEEDED, CHOPPED FINELY

1½ TEASPOONS BLACK SESAME SEEDS

1 Combine hoisin sauce and sesame oil in a medium bowl, add tofu; carefully toss to coat. Set aside.

2 Combine carrot and cucumber in a medium bowl with vinegar; season with salt. Stand for 20 minutes. Drain; reserve pickling liquid.

3 Blanch broccolini and wombok, separately, in boiling water then refresh in a bowl of iced water; drain. Cut broccolini in half lengthways, then into strips.

4 Place wombok leaves on a flat board. Divide tofu, pickled vegetables, broccolini, green onion and herbs in centre of each leaf. Roll up to enclose filling, secure with toothpicks.

5 Place 1 tablespoon of the reserved pickling liquid in a small bowl with rice malt syrup, fish sauce and chilli; stir to combine.

6 Serve wraps with dipping sauce, sprinkled with sesame seeds.

prep + cook time 40 minutes (+ standing & cooling)
serves 4 (makes 8 wraps)
nutritional count per serving 4.8g total fat (0.6g saturated fat); 788kJ (188 cal); 18.3g carbohydrate; 13g protein; 9.4g fibre

I AM
LOW FAT
VEGETARIAN
RAW

I AM
LOW CARB
VEGETARIAN
LOW FAT

YOU CAN USE ANY OTHER VARIETY OF BEAN INSTEAD OF THE BUTTER BEANS. THIS SALAD IS GREAT BOTH WARM AND COOL.

ROASTED CARROT
And BUTTER BEAN SALAD

8 SHALLOTS (200G), PEELED, HALVED

1 TABLESPOON OLIVE OIL

430G (14 OUNCES) BABY CARROTS, TRIMMED, RESERVED CARROT TOPS

400G (12½ OUNCES) CANNED BUTTER BEANS, DRAINED, RINSED

1 TEASPOON DIJON MUSTARD

2 TABLESPOONS LEMON JUICE

1 TEASPOON RICE MALT SYRUP

1 CUP (100G) WATERCRESS

1 Preheat oven to 200°C/400°F. Line an oven tray with baking paper.

2 Place shallots on tray; drizzle with half the oil. Season. Cover with foil; roast for 30 minutes or until tender.

3 Remove foil. Add carrots and butter beans to tray; drizzle with remaining oil, then toss to coat. Roast, uncovered, for 20 minutes or until carrots are tender.

4 Chop ⅓ cup of the reserved carrot tops; place in a small bowl with mustard, juice and rice malt syrup. Stir to combine.

5 Place roasted carrot mixture in a serving bowl with dressing, watercress and 1 cup of the remaining reserved carrot tops; toss gently to combine.

prep + cook time 1 hour (+ cooling) **serves** 4
nutritional count per serving 5g total fat (0.7g saturated fat); 490kJ (117 cal); 9.5g carbohydrate; 4.9g protein; 7.8g fibre

FALAFEL SCOTCH EGGS
With GREEN TAHINI

400G (12½ OUNCES) CANNED CHICKPEAS (GARBANZO BEANS), DRAINED, RINSED

400G (12½ OUNCES) CANNED CANNELLINI BEANS, DRAINED, RINSED

¼ CUP (35G) PLAIN (ALL-PURPOSE) FLOUR

2 GREEN ONIONS (SCALLIONS), CHOPPED

1 TABLESPOON RAS EL HANOUT

4 FREE-RANGE EGGS

¼ CUP (35G) SESAME SEEDS

VEGETABLE OIL, FOR SHALLOW-FRYING

2 BABY COS (ROMAINE) LETTUCE (180G), QUARTERED

250G (8 OUNCES) HEIRLOOM CHERRY TOMATOES, HALVED

GREEN TAHINI

1 CUP CHOPPED FRESH MINT

½ CUP (140G) GREEK-STYLE YOGHURT

¼ CUP (60ML) LEMON JUICE

¼ CUP (70G) TAHINI PASTE

1 TABLESPOON CIDER VINEGAR

½ SMALL CLOVE GARLIC, CRUSHED

1 Process chickpeas, cannellini beans, flour, green onion and ras el hanout in a food processor to form a coarse paste. Season. Refrigerate for 30 minutes or until firm.

2 Meanwhile, place eggs in a small saucepan with enough cold water to cover. Bring to the boil. Reduce heat; simmer, uncovered, for 4 minutes for soft boiled. Drain; rinse under cold water then peel. Pat dry with paper towel.

3 Shape a quarter of the chickpea mixture around each egg. Sprinkle with sesame seeds to lightly coat. Refrigerate for 30 minutes.

4 Heat oil to a medium frying pan over medium heat; shallow-fry scotch eggs for 5 minutes, turning on all sides until golden and crisp. Drain on paper towel.

5 Make green tahini.

6 Serve scotch eggs with lettuce and tomatoes; drizzle with green tahini. Season.

green tahini Blend ingredients until smooth. Thin with a little water if necessary. Season.

prep + cook time 30 minutes (+ refrigeration) **serves** 4
nutritional count per serving 43g total fat (7.3g saturated fat); 2488kJ (594 cal); 25.5g carbohydrate; 22g protein; 10.8g fibre

tip For a gluten-free option, use chickpea flour (besan) or rice flour instead of plain (all-purpose) flour.

I AM
VEGETARIAN
PROTEIN RICH
HIGH FIBRE

SMOKED TROUT IS AVAILABLE AT MOST SUPERMARKETS
IN VARIOUS SIZED FILLETED PORTIONS. THESE SANDWICHES
ARE BEST ASSEMBLED JUST BEFORE SERVING.

OPEN RYE SANDWICH
with SMOKED TROUT And CHERRY SALAD

2 TABLESPOONS RAW BUCKWHEAT

1 SMOKED TROUT (300G), SKINNED, BONED, FLAKED COARSELY

150G (4½ OUNCES) FRESH CHERRIES, PITTED, SQUASHED

½ SMALL RED ONION (50G), SLICED THINLY

¾ CUP LOOSELY PACKED FRESH DILL

1 TABLESPOON LEMON JUICE

1 TABLESPOON EXTRA VIRGIN OLIVE OIL

4 SLICES RYE BREAD (180G)

1 MEDIUM AVOCADO (250G)

1 Place buckwheat in a small dry frying pan; cook, stirring, over high heat for 1 minute or until browned lightly.

2 Combine trout, cherries, onion, dill, juice and 3 teaspoons of the oil in a large bowl; season.

3 Toast bread until browned lightly; spread avocado on slices. Spoon trout mixture on bread; top with buckwheat and remaining oil.

prep + cook time 25 minutes **serves** 2
nutritional count per serving 34.7g total fat (7g saturated fat); 3010kJ (719 cal); 60.5g carbohydrate; 34.6g protein; 12.9g fibre

PRAWN SALAD
with DAIKON And CUCUMBER

1KG (2 POUNDS) COOKED MEDIUM PRAWNS
(SHRIMP)

¼ CUP (60G) COCONUT OIL

½ CUP (50G) SHAVED FRESH COCONUT
(SEE TIPS)

½ SMALL DAIKON (200G), CUT INTO
THIN MATCHSTICKS

2 LEBANESE CUCUMBER (260G),
CUT INTO THIN MATCHSTICKS

½ CUP (75G) ROASTED SALTED CASHEWS

1 CUP LOOSELY PACKED FRESH CORIANDER
(CILANTRO) LEAVES

1 CUP LOOSELY PACKED FRESH MINT LEAVES

LIME CHEEKS, TO SERVE

COCONUT MILK DRESSING

1 TEASPOON FINELY GRATED PALM SUGAR

⅔ CUP (160ML) COCONUT MILK

1 TABLESPOON LIME JUICE

3 TEASPOONS FISH SAUCE

1 Peel and devein prawns, leaving tails intact.

2 Make coconut milk dressing.

3 Heat coconut oil in a medium frying pan over high heat.
Add shaved coconut; cook, stirring occasionally, for
2 minutes or until golden brown. Drain on paper towel.

4 Place prawns and toasted coconut in a large bowl
with daikon, cucumber, cashews and herbs; toss gently
to combine. Just before serving, drizzle with dressing;
serve with lime.

coconut milk dressing Place ingredients in a screw-top
jar; shake well. Season to taste. Refrigerate until needed.

prep + cook time 35 minutes **serves** 4
nutritional count per serving 38.1g total fat (26.2g
saturated fat); 2593kJ (619 cal); 9.4g carbohydrate;
57.4g protein; 5.4g fibre

tips To save time, buy peeled prawns; you will need
500g (1 pound). To shave flesh from a fresh coconut,
wrap the coconut in an old, clean tea towel and firmly
hit the coconut on a hard floor, ideally outside and
close to a bowl to catch the coconut water. Separate
and discard the hard outer shell of the coconut. Use a
vegetable peeler to shave the flesh. Keep the dressing
separate until just before serving. Dressing can be made
up to 2 days ahead; keep refrigerated. Store leftover
coconut milk in an airtight container in the fridge
for up to 3 days. It's a great addition to smoothies or
drizzled over fruit.

I AM
IRON RICH
PROTEIN RICH
LOW GI

I AM
GLUTEN FREE
PROTEIN RICH
LOW CARB

BEETROOT FRITTATAS
WITH MIXED HERB SALAD

10 FREE-RANGE EGGS

500G (1 POUND) COOKED, PEELED BEETROOT (BEETS), CHOPPED COARSELY

¼ CUP COARSELY CHOPPED FRESH DILL

½ CUP (55G) COARSELY CHOPPED ROASTED WALNUTS

2 TABLESPOONS OLIVE OIL

MIXED HERB SALAD

1 TABLESPOON SUNFLOWER SEED KERNELS

3 TEASPOONS BLACK CHIA SEEDS

½ SMALL RED ONION (50G), SLICED THINLY

⅔ CUP FRESH FLAT-LEAF PARSLEY LEAVES

⅔ CUP FRESH MINT LEAVES

2 TABLESPOONS SMALL FRESH TARRAGON LEAVES

2 TABLESPOONS FRESH DILL SPRIGS

1 TABLESPOON EXTRA VIRGIN OLIVE OIL

1 TABLESPOON LEMON JUICE

1 Preheat oven to 180°C/350°F. Grease 8 holes of two 6-hole (¾-cup/180ml) texas muffin pans; line bases with baking paper.

2 Whisk eggs in a medium bowl. Stir in beetroot, dill, walnuts and oil until combined; season. Divide mixture into pan holes.

3 Bake frittatas for 20 minutes or until a sharp knife inserted into the centre comes out clean.

4 Meanwhile, make mixed herb salad.

5 Serve frittatas with salad.

mixed herb salad Heat a large frying pan over medium heat; cook seeds, stirring, for 2 minutes or until toasted. Place seeds in a medium bowl with remaining ingredients; toss gently to combine.

prep + cook time 40 minutes **serves** 4 (makes 8)
nutritional count per serving 37.7g total fat (7g saturated fat); 2027kJ (484 cal); 10.4g carbohydrate; 22.8g protein; 8.5g fibre
tip Frittatas are great to pack for work or school lunch.

THESE MEATZZAS ARE GLUTEN- AND DAIRY-FREE. USE A MICROPLANE TO GRATE MACADAMIAS. BASES CAN BE SHAPED, THEN FROZEN UNCOOKED IN AN AIRTIGHT CONTAINER FOR UP TO 3 MONTHS.

SPINACH *And* EGGPLANT

MINI MEATZZAS

500G (1 POUND) LEAN MINCED (GROUND) BEEF

1 FREE-RANGE EGG, BEATEN LIGHTLY

1 SMALL RED ONION (100G), GRATED COARSELY

1 CLOVE GARLIC, CRUSHED

¼ CUP (30G) GROUND ALMONDS

1 TABLESPOON FINELY CHOPPED FRESH FLAT-LEAF PARSLEY

½ TEASPOON FINELY CHOPPED FRESH ROSEMARY

⅓ CUP (95G) TOMATO PASTE

30G (1 OUNCE) BABY SPINACH LEAVES

3 BABY EGGPLANTS (180G), SLICED THINLY CROSSWAYS

2 TABLESPOONS EXTRA VIRGIN OLIVE OIL

15G (½ OUNCE) MICRO PARSLEY

5 MACADAMIAS

1 Preheat oven to 220°C/425°F. Line two large oven trays with baking paper.

2 Combine beef, egg, onion, garlic, ground almonds and herbs in a large bowl; season. Roll 2 level tablespoons of mixture into balls, flatten into 9cm (3¾-inch) rounds; place on trays.

3 Spread tomato paste on rounds; top with spinach and eggplant. Drizzle with oil; season.

4 Bake for 15 minutes or until bases are cooked through. Top with micro-parsley and finely grated macadamias.

prep + cook time 40 minutes **makes** 12

nutritional count per meatzzas 10g total fat (2.7g saturated fat); 634kJ (151 cal); 1.7g carbohydrate; 12.9g protein; 1.3g fibre

SNACKS

FRUIT & NUT CHOCOLATE CLUSTERS

prep + cook time 15 minutes (+ refrigeration)

makes 12

Melt 100g (3oz) chopped dark chocolate (85% cocoa) in a medium heatproof bowl over a saucepan of simmering water. Remove from heat; stir in ½ cup (70g) dried blueberries, ½ cup (70g) chopped seeded fresh dates, ½ cup (95g) coarsely chopped dried figs, ½ cup (80g) sultanas and ¼ cup (35g) chopped roasted pistachios. Drop spoonfuls of mixture in clusters on a baking-paper-lined oven tray. Sprinkle with ¼ cup (35g) chopped roasted pistachios. Refrigerate until firm.

SWEET DUKKAH

prep + cook time 25 minutes (+ cooling)

makes 1 cup

Preheat oven to 180°C/350°F. Roast ⅓ cup (55g) almond kernels on an oven tray for 3 minutes. Add 2 tablespoons sesame seeds to tray, roast a further 5 minutes or until fragrant and golden. Add ⅓ cup (45g) shelled pistachios to tray; roast for a further 1 minute. Cool. Process roasted nut mixture with 2 tablespoons coconut sugar, 2 teaspoons ground cinnamon, ½ teaspoon ground ginger and ½ teaspoon mixed spice, using pulse button until nuts are finely chopped. Serve dukkah sprinkled over greek-style yoghurt and torn fresh figs.

COCONUT OAT COOKIES

prep + cook time 45 minutes (+ cooling)

makes 20

Preheat oven to 150°C/300°F. Combine ⅓ cup (60g) steel-cut oats, 1 cup (75g) desiccated coconut, ⅔ cup (110g) coconut sugar, ½ cup (70g) LSA and 2 tablespoons honey in a large bowl. Melt ¼ cup (60g) coconut oil in a small saucepan. Combine ½ teaspoon bicarbonate of soda (baking soda) and 2 tablespoons boiling water in a small bowl. Add melted coconut oil and soda mixture to dry ingredients; mix well. Press level tablespoons of mixture into balls; place 5cm (2in) apart on baking-paper-lined oven trays, flatten lightly. Bake for 20 minutes or until golden. Cool on trays.

CHOCOLATE-DIPPED STRAWBERRIES

prep + cook time 15 minutes (+ cooling)

makes 12

Preheat oven to 180°C/350°F. Roast ⅓ cup (35g) walnuts on an oven tray for 5 minutes or until golden. Chop coarsely; cool. Melt 75g (2½oz) chopped dark chocolate (85% cocoa) in a small heatproof bowl over a saucepan of simmering water. Cool for 3 minutes. Half-dip 250g (8oz) strawberries in melted chocolate, one at a time; drain away excess. Place strawberries on a baking-paper-lined oven tray. Sprinkle with chopped nuts before chocolate sets.

I AM
PROTEIN RICH
HIGH IN CALCIUM
VEGETARIAN

MUHAMMARA CAN BE SERVED ON ITS OWN AS A SNACK WITH VEGIE STICKS, EITHER WARM OR AT ROOM TEMPERATURE. POMEGRANATE MOLASSES IS AVAILABLE AT MIDDLE EASTERN FOOD STORES, SPECIALTY FOOD SHOPS AND SOME DELICATESSENS.

KALE TARTS
WITH MUHAMMARA

6 SHEETS FILLO PASTRY (120G)

2 TABLESPOONS OLIVE OIL

2 TABLESPOONS WHITE CHIA SEEDS

4 GREEN ONIONS (SCALLIONS), CHOPPED

80G (2½ OUNCES) BABY KALE LEAVES

400G (12½ OUNCES) CANNED CHICKPEAS (GARBANZO BEANS), DRAINED, RINSED

1 CLOVE GARLIC, CRUSHED

150G (4½ OUNCES) RICOTTA, CRUMBLED

125G (4 OUNCES) HALOUMI, CHOPPED

2 TEASPOONS CHOPPED FRESH DILL, PLUS EXTRA, TO SERVE

MUHAMMARA

¾ CUP (180G) BOTTLED ROASTED RED CAPSICUM (BELL PEPPER), DRAINED, RESERVING 1 TABLESPOON OIL

½ CUP (50G) TOASTED WALNUTS

1 TABLESPOON POMEGRANATE MOLASSES

1 TABLESPOON LEMON JUICE

1 Preheat oven to 200°C/400°F. Lightly grease a 6-hole (¾-cup/180ml) texas muffin pan.

2 Layer pastry sheets, brushing between each layer with 1 teaspoon oil and sprinkling with 1 teaspoon chia seeds. Cut pastry stack into six equal squares. Gently ease one stack into each muffin hole. Bake for 5 minutes. Reduce oven to 160°C/325°F.

3 Meanwhile, heat remaining oil in a large frying pan over medium heat; cook green onion, stirring for 3 minutes or until soft. Stir in kale, chickpeas and garlic; cook, stirring for 2 minutes or until kale has wilted. Transfer mixture to a large heatproof bowl; gently stir in ricotta, haloumi and dill until combined. Spoon kale mixture into pastry cases.

4 Bake for 20 minutes or until pastry is crisp and golden.

5 Meanwhile, make muhammara.

6 Serve tarts topped with muhammara and extra dill.

muhammara Process capsicum and reserved oil with walnuts, molasses and juice until smooth.

prep + cook time 45 minutes **serves** 6

nutritional count per serving 24.7g total fat (6.3g saturated fat); 1631kJ (390 cal); 24.5g carbohydrate; 14.8g protein; 5.7g fibre

serving suggestion Serve with a green salad.

STORE DRESSING IN A SMALL SEPARATE AIRTIGHT CONTAINER.
YOU WILL NEED 2 CUPS OF COOKED BROWN RICE.

BURRITO
SALAD BOWL

400G (12½ OUNCES) CANNED BLACK BEANS, DRAINED, RINSED

2 GREEN ONIONS (SCALLIONS), CHOPPED FINELY

2 TABLESPOONS LIME JUICE

2 BABY COS (ROMAINE) LETTUCE HEARTS, QUARTERED

200G (6½ OUNCES) SHREDDED RED CABBAGE

4 BABY RADISHES (120G), TRIMMED, SLICED THINLY

1 TABLESPOON EXTRA VIRGIN OLIVE OIL

250G (8-OUNCE) PACKET MICROWAVE BROWN RICE

1 CUP (280G) GREEK-STYLE YOGHURT

2 TEASPOONS CHIPOTLE CHILLI SAUCE

250G (8 OUNCES) MINI ROMA (EGG) TOMATOES

1 MEDIUM AVOCADO (250G), SLICED

½ CUP FRESH CORIANDER (CILANTRO) SPRIGS

LIME WEDGES, TO SERVE

SPICED PEPITAS

½ CUP (100G) PEPITAS (PUMPKIN SEED KERNELS)

1 TABLESPOON OLIVE OIL

1 TABLESPOON PURE MAPLE SYRUP

½ TEASPOONS CAYENNE PEPPER

1 Combine beans, green onion and juice in a small bowl; season to taste.

2 Place lettuce, cabbage, radish and oil in a large bowl; toss gently to combine.

3 Heat rice in microwave according to packet directions.

4 Make spiced pepitas.

5 Combine yoghurt and chill sauce in a small jug.

6 Divide rice, bean mixture and cabbage salad among bowls. Top with tomatoes, avocado, spiced pepitas and coriander. Serve with yoghurt dressing and lime wedges.

spiced pepitas Stir ingredients in a hot frying pan until pepitas are popped and lightly browned. Cool.

prep + cook time 30 minutes **serves** 4

nutritional count per serving 36.9g total fat (8.5g saturated fat); 2778kJ (664 cal); 53g carbohydrate; 22g protein; 14.9g fibre

I AM
EGG FREE
PROTEIN RICH
LOW GI

I AM
GLUTEN FREE
PROTEIN RICH
DAIRY FREE

KOHLRABI KUMARA ROSTI
WITH CASHEW DIP

You will need to soak the cashews for the dip in water for 3 hours before you start this recipe.

350G (11 OUNCES) KOHLRABI, SHREDDED

200G (6 OUNCES) KUMARA (ORANGE SWEET POTATO), GRATED COARSELY

¼ CUP (40G) BROWN RICE FLOUR

3 GREEN ONIONS (SCALLIONS), SLICED THINLY

1 CUP LOOSELY PACKED FRESH CORIANDER (CILANTRO), CHOPPED

¼ CUP (35G) LSA (SEE TIPS)

3 FREE-RANGE EGG WHITES

1 TABLESPOON WATER

2 TABLESPOONS OLIVE OIL

CASHEW DIP

¾ CUP (120G) DRY ROASTED CASHEWS

1 CLOVE GARLIC, CRUSHED

1 TEASPOON FINELY GRATED LEMON RIND

2 TABLESPOONS LEMON JUICE

½ CUP (125ML) WATER

¼ CUP LOOSELY PACKED FRESH MINT LEAVES, SHREDDED FINELY

1 Make cashew dip.

2 Combine kohlrabi, kumara, brown rice flour, green onion, coriander, LSA and combined egg whites and the water; mix well. Season. Shape mixture into 8 portions.

3 Heat half the oil in a large frying pan over medium-high heat; cook rösti, in two batches, for 5 minutes each side or until golden.

4 Serve rösti with cashew dip.

cashew dip Soak cashews in water for 3 hours; drain. Place drained cashews in a high-powered blender with garlic, rind, juice and the water; blend until smooth. Season to taste. Just before serving, stir in mint.

prep + cook time 40 minutes (+ soaking) **serves** 4
nutritional count per serving 28.8g total fat (4.3g saturated fat); 1881kJ (449 cal); 28.3g carbohydrate; 15.9g protein; 9.1g fibre
tips LSA is a ground mixture of linseeds (L), sunflower seeds (S) and almonds (A); available from supermarkets and health food stores. Rösti can be made a day ahead; store, covered, in the fridge.

BROCCOLI *And* PRAWN FRIED RICE

¼ CUP (60ML) REDUCED-SALT SOY SAUCE

2 TABLESPOONS LIME JUICE

1 TABLESPOON FINELY GRATED FRESH GINGER

1 FRESH LONG RED CHILLI, SLICED THINLY

1 CLOVE GARLIC, CRUSHED

500G (1 POUND) LARGE UNCOOKED PRAWNS (SHRIMP)

1 TABLESPOON COCONUT OIL

2 FREE-RANGE EGGS, BEATEN LIGHTLY

500G (1 POUND) BROCCOLI, CUT INTO FLORETS, STEMS CHOPPED

4 GREEN ONIONS (SCALLIONS), SLICED THINLY

1 MEDIUM CARROT (120G), GRATED COARSELY

1 TABLESPOON REDUCED-SALT SOY SAUCE, EXTRA

½ CUP (75G) ROASTED CASHEWS, CHOPPED COARSELY

⅓ CUP FRESH CORIANDER (CILANTRO) LEAVES

LIME CHEEKS, TO SERVE

1 Whisk soy sauce, juice, ginger, chilli and garlic in a medium bowl. Peel and devein prawns, leaving tails intact; cut in half lengthways. Add prawns to bowl; toss to combine in soy mixture.

2 Heat 1 teaspoon of the coconut oil in a wok over high heat. Pour egg into wok; cook, tilting wok, until almost set. Remove omelette from wok; roll tightly, slice thinly.

3 Place broccoli in a food processor; pulse until finely chopped and it resembles rice.

4 Heat remaining coconut oil in wok over high heat. Add green onion and carrot; stir-fry for 5 minutes or until tender. Add prawn mixture; stir-fry for 5 minutes until just cooked. Add broccoli and extra soy sauce; stir-fry for 2 minutes.

5 Serve fried rice topped with cashews, coriander, omelette and lime cheeks.

prep + cook time 30 minutes **serves** 4

nutritional count per serving 17g total fat (6.7g saturated fat); 1273kJ (304 cal); 6.8g carbohydrate; 26.7g protein; 7.5g fibre

tip Fried rice is best made just before serving.

I AM
PROTEIN RICH
MINERAL RICH
LOW FAT

27

EGGPLANT NOODLE SALAD

WITH SMOKED TROUT

1 MEDIUM EGGPLANT (300G), HALVED LENGTHWAYS, CUT INTO WEDGES

1 TABLESPOON PEANUT OIL

270G (8½ OUNCES) GREEN TEA NOODLES

¼ CUP (60ML) RICE VINEGAR

¼ CUP (60ML) LEMON JUICE

2 TABLESPOONS REDUCED-SALT SOY SAUCE

1 TABLESPOON HONEY

1 TABLESPOON FINELY GRATED FRESH GINGER

1 TABLESPOON SESAME OIL

200G (6½ OUNCES) GREEN BEANS, TRIMMED, HALVED

2 GREEN ONIONS (SCALLIONS), SLICED THINLY

2 TABLESPOONS SESAME SEEDS, TOASTED

180G (5½-OUNCE) PIECE SMOKED TROUT, FLAKED

1 GREEN ONION (SCALLION), EXTRA, SLICED

1 Brush eggplant with peanut oil. Cook eggplant, on a heated oiled grill plate (or grill or barbecue) over medium-high heat for 2 minutes each side or until tender. Transfer to plate.

2 Meanwhile, cook noodles according to packet directions. Drain, rinse.

3 Place vinegar, juice, soy sauce, honey, ginger and sesame oil in a screw-top jar; shake well.

4 Boil, steam or microwave beans until tender; cool.

5 Place eggplant, noodles and beans in a large bowl with green onion, half the sesame seeds and the dressing; toss gently to combine. Divide mixture into serving bowls; top with flaked trout, remaining sesame seeds and extra green onion.

prep + cook time 25 minutes **serves** 4
nutritional count per serving 16.7g total fat (2.4g saturated fat); 2034kJ (487 cal); 56.2g carbohydrate; 26.1g protein; 7.7g fibre

tips Smoked trout is available at most supermarkets in various sized filleted portions. Salad is best made just before serving.

SUPER SALADS

TO BUILD THE PERFECT SUPER SALAD, START WITH LEAFY GREENS, COLOURFUL VEGIES AND GRAINS. ADD EGGS, CHICKEN, LEAN MEAT OR LEGUMES FOR PROTEIN, THEN TOP WITH CITRUS AND A HANDFUL OF NUTS OR SEEDS.

RAINBOW SALAD
WITH TAHINI And CUMIN DRESSING

1 LEBANESE CUCUMBER (130G), SLICED THINLY

400G (12½ OUNCES) CANNED CHICKPEAS (GARBANZO BEANS), DRAINED, RINSED

1 MEDIUM CARROT (120G), CUT INTO THIN MATCHSTICKS

1 LARGE BEETROOT (BEETS) (200G), PEELED, CUT INTO THIN MATCHSTICKS

4 BABY COS (ROMAINE) LETTUCE LEAVES

½ TEASPOON POPPY SEEDS

TAHINI & CUMIN DRESSING

2 TABLESPOONS TAHINI

2 TABLESPOONS LEMON JUICE

2 TABLESPOONS GREEK-STYLE YOGHURT

1 TABLESPOON OLIVE OIL

½ TEASPOON GROUND CUMIN

1 TABLESPOON WARM WATER, APPROXIMATELY

1 Make tahini and cumin dressing.

2 Spoon half the dressing into four 1½ cup (375ml) glass jars; top with cucumber, chickpeas, carrot, beetroot and lettuce. Drizzle with remaining dressing, sprinkle with poppy seeds.

tahini & cumin dressing Stir tahini, juice, yoghurt, oil and cumin in a jug. Whisk in enough of the warm water until smooth; season to taste.

prep time 20 minutes **serves** 4

nutritional count per serving 13.2g total fat (2.1g saturated fat); 1027kJ (245 cal); 17.4g carbohydrate; 9.9g protein; 9.8g fibre

tip Dress salad just before serving to prevent the beetroot bleeding into the other vegetables.

I AM
EGG FREE
HIGH IN IRON
LOW FAT

I AM
NUT FREE
PROTEIN RICH
LOW GI

POACHED CHICKEN
QUINOA *And* WATERCRESS SALAD

500G (1 POUND) CHICKEN BREAST FILLETS, TRIMMED, HALVED HORIZONTALLY

1 CUP (200G) TRI-COLOURED QUINOA

2 CUPS (500ML) WATER

2 CUPS (60G) PICKED WATERCRESS SPRIGS

6 TRIMMED WATERMELON RADISHES (90G), SLICED THINLY

1 SMALL AVOCADO (200G), SLICED THINLY

¼ CUP (50G) PEPITAS (PUMPKIN SEED KERNELS)

BALSAMIC DRESSING

¼ CUP (60ML) OLIVE OIL

1½ TABLESPOONS LEMON JUICE

2 TEASPOONS BALSAMIC VINEGAR

2 TEASPOONS PURE MAPLE SYRUP

2 TEASPOONS DIJON MUSTARD

1 Place chicken in a medium saucepan and cover with water; bring to the boil. Reduce heat to low; simmer, uncovered, for 10 minutes or until cooked. Cool chicken in poaching liquid for 10 minutes; drain, then slice thinly.

2 Meanwhile, rinse quinoa well; drain. Place quinoa and the water in a medium saucepan; bring to the boil. Reduce heat to low; simmer, covered, for 10 minutes or until quinoa is tender. Refresh under cold running water. Drain, pressing quinoa with the back of a spoon to remove as much liquid as possible.

3 Make balsamic dressing.

4 Place chicken and quinoa in a large bowl with remaining ingredients and dressing; toss to combine.

balsamic dressing Stir ingredients in a small jug; season to taste.

prep + cook time 30 minutes **serves** 4

nutritional count per serving 38.3g total fat (7.4g saturated fat); 2743kJ (655 cal); 39.2g carbohydrate; 38g protein; 5.5g fibre

tip We used tri-colour quinoa, but you could use white, black or red.

POMEGRANATE MOLASSES IS AVAILABLE AT MIDDLE EASTERN FOOD STORES, SPECIALTY FOOD SHOPS AND SOME DELICATESSENS. THIS SALAD CAN BE SERVED WARM OR COLD.

ROASTED CAULIFLOWER *And* SPICED CHICKPEA SALAD

1 SMALL CAULIFLOWER (680G), TRIMMED, SLICED

220G (7 OUNCES) BRUSSELS SPROUTS, TRIMMED, SLICED

2 TABLESPOONS OLIVE OIL

400G (12½ OUNCES) CANNED CHICKPEAS (GARBANZO BEANS), DRAINED, RINSED

1 TEASPOON SMOKED PAPRIKA

1 TEASPOON GROUND CUMIN

1 TEASPOON GROUND CORIANDER

12 CAVOLO NERO (TUSCAN CABBAGE) LEAVES (120G), TRIMMED, TORN

TAHINI DRESSING

1 TABLESPOON TAHINI

1 TABLESPOON POMEGRANATE MOLASSES

1 FRESH LONG RED CHILLI, SEEDED, CHOPPED FINELY

1 SMALL CLOVE GARLIC, CRUSHED

¼ CUP (60ML) WATER

1 Preheat oven to 200°C/400°F.

2 Place cauliflower and brussels sprouts on an oven tray; drizzle with half the oil. Season; toss to coat. Place chickpeas on another oven tray; sprinkle with paprika, cumin and coriander. Season; drizzle with remaining oil.

3 Roast vegetables and chickpeas for 25 minutes. Add cavolo nero to vegetables; roast a further 5 minutes or until vegetables are tender and chickpeas are crisp.

4 Meanwhile, make tahini dressing.

5 Serve vegetables and chickpeas drizzled with dressing.

tahini dressing Combine ingredients in a small bowl.

prep + cook time 40 minutes **serves** 4

nutritional count per serving 14.4g total fat (2.1g saturated fat); 1164kJ (278 cal); 19.5g carbohydrate; 11.5g protein; 11.7g fibre

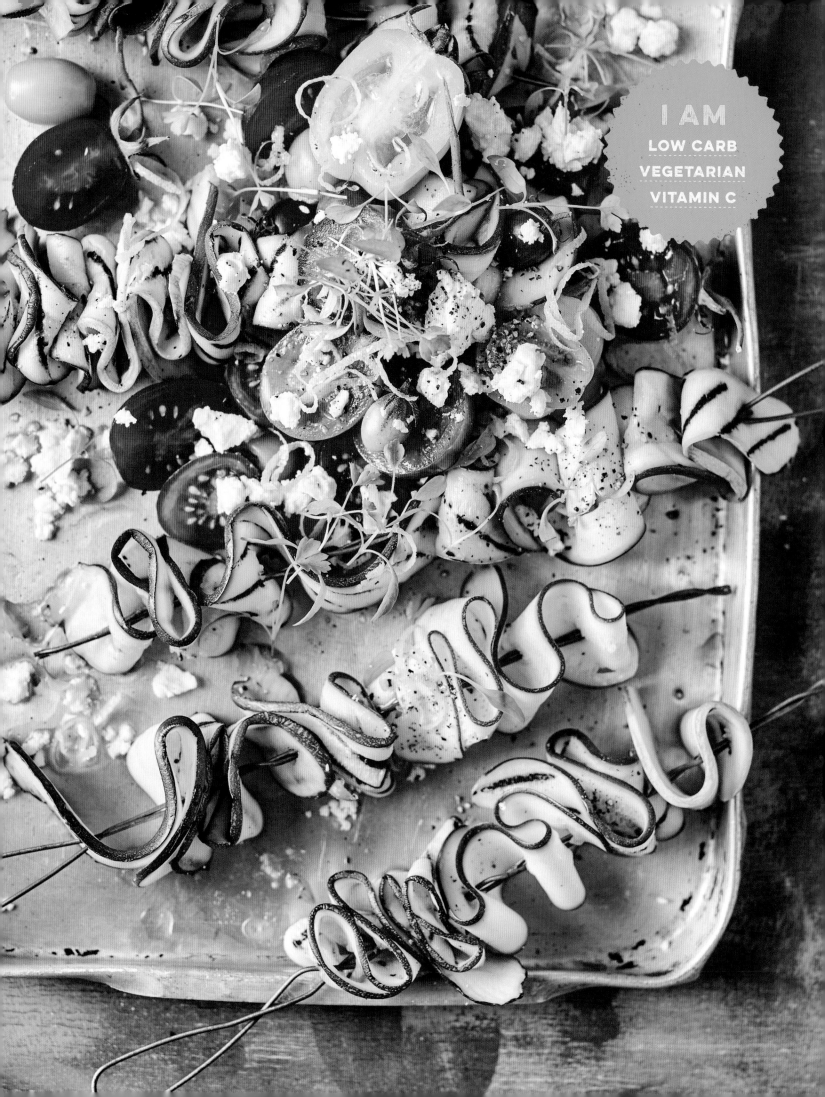

ZUCCHINI RIBBON SKEWERS
with TOMATO And FETTA SALAD

3 MEDIUM ZUCCHINI (360G)

125G (4 OUNCES) CHERRY TOMATOES, HALVED

125G (4 OUNCES) FETTA, CRUMBLED

¼ CUP COARSELY CHOPPED FRESH FLAT-LEAF PARSLEY

2 TEASPOONS COARSELY GRATED LEMON RIND

2 TABLESPOONS EXTRA VIRGIN OLIVE OIL

1½ TABLESPOONS LEMON JUICE

1 Cut zucchini lengthways into ribbons; thread ribbons onto 12 skewers.

2 Cook zucchini skewers on heated oiled grill plate (or grill or barbecue), for 30 seconds each side or until lightly charred and just tender.

3 Combine tomato, fetta, parsley and rind on a platter. Top with skewers, drizzle with combined oil and juice.

prep + cook time 25 minutes **serves** 4

nutritional count per serving 16.5g total fat (6.1g saturated fat); 773kJ (185 cal); 1.9g carbohydrate; 6.4g protein; 1.6g fibre

tip Use a vegetable peeler to cut the zucchini into long thin ribbons.

BUTTERNUT PUMPKIN

This pear-shaped buff-skinned pumpkin is the best all-rounder pumpkin due to its lower moisture content. Try it in soups, curries, roasted and pureed. The rounded bottom half of the pumpkin yields the least flesh as it is mostly hollow and contains the seeds. For maximum flesh choose those with long, thick necks and relatively small bottom halves.

QUEENSLAND BLUE

This large orange-fleshed pumpkin has a particularly hard skin while the flesh is quite moist making it a favourite for mashing and for scones, but also suitable for roasting.

AUSTRALIAN BUTTER PUMPKIN

This heirloom variety can be found at farmers markets and specialist green grocers. The hard-shelled fruit (pumpkin is classified as one) has fine sweet tasting flesh. Look out for other heirloom types – gramma, buttercup and golden nugget.

JAP PUMPKIN

Is the abbreviated name for Japanese pumpkin or kobocha, as it is called in Japan. There are many varieties of this medium-sized yellow-orange fleshed pumpkin such as Kent. The relatively dry flesh is excellent roasted, or chargrilled and all parts, skin and seeds, are edible.

WHY ORANGE?

The compound that makes orange-coloured vegetables orange is beta-carotene, which can be converted to vitamin A in the body. Other carotenoid-rich vegetables are: sweet potato and carrot, and fruits include apricots, pawpaw and oranges. Less obvious sources are leafy green vegetables such as kale and spinach and broccoli, in these vegetables the green pigment chlorophyll disguises the carotene colour.

Pumpkins

ARE WINTER-GROWING MEMBERS OF THE CUCURBITA GENUS THAT INCLUDES CUCUMBERS, ZUCCHINI AND MELONS. THE FAST-GROWING VINES CREEP ALONG THE GROUND SO THE PUMPKIN'S WEIGHT IS NOT SUPPORTED. THE TENDER YOUNG LEAVES OF THE VINE ARE EDIBLE AND MAY BE EATEN IN SALADS OR STIR-FRIED, AS TOO ARE THE FLOWERS.

PUMPKINS ARE 90% WATER MAKING THEM LOW KILOJOULE; THEY CONTAIN MORE FIBRE THAN KALE AND MORE POTASSIUM THAN BANANAS.

Pepitas (PUMPKIN SEEDS) ARE A GOOD SOURCE OF PROTEIN, VITAMINS, MINERALS AND OMEGA-3 FATTY ACIDS; 100G OF SEEDS PROVIDE 110% OF THE DAILY REQUIREMENT OF IRON.

PUMPKIN

I AM

IRON RICH
HIGH IN FIBRE
LOW CARB

MOST VEGETABLES, ESPECIALLY *colourful* ONES, HAVE SUPERFOOD PROPERTIES. PUMPKIN IS NO EXCEPTION, WITH 100G CONTAINING 246% OF OUR DAILY REQUIREMENT FOR *Vitamin A.* THIS POWERFUL *antioxidant* IS NEEDED FOR SKIN HEALTH AND GOOD EYE SIGHT.

USE A MANDOLINE OR V-SLICER TO CUT THE FENNEL INTO WAFER THIN SLICES. USE A MIXTURE OF ORANGES AND BLOOD ORANGES WHEN THEY ARE IN SEASON.

ORANGE, FENNEL  HAZELNUT SALAD

1 RUBY GRAPEFRUIT (400G)

2 MEDIUM ORANGES (480G)

3 BABY FENNEL BULBS (390G), SLICED THINLY, FRONDS RESERVED

1 RED WITLOF (230G), LEAVES SEPARATED

2 TABLESPOONS SKINLESS HAZELNUTS, ROASTED, CHOPPED FINELY

2 TABLESPOONS BABY FRESH FLAT-LEAF PARSLEY

2 TABLESPOONS FINELY CHOPPED FRESH MINT LEAVES

1 FRESH LONG RED CHILLI, SEEDED, CHOPPED FINELY

1½ TABLESPOONS OLIVE OIL

1 TABLESPOON WHITE BALSAMIC VINEGAR

½ TEASPOON FENNEL SEEDS, CRUSHED FINELY

1 Use a small sharp knife to cut the top and bottom from grapefruit and oranges. Cut off the rind with the white pith, following the curve of the fruit. Hold grapefruit over a bowl to catch the juices, then cut down both sides of the white membrane to release each segment. Reserve juice; you need 1 tablespoon. Cut oranges into slices.

2 Arrange grapefruit, orange, sliced fennel and witlof on a serving plate. Scatter with hazelnuts, herbs and chilli.

3 Whisk oil, vinegar and fennel seeds into reserved juice; season to taste.

4 Serve salad drizzled with dressing and topped with reserved fennel fronds.

prep time 30 minutes **serves** 4

nutritional count per serving 10.6g total fat (1.2g saturated fat); 729kJ (174 cal); 12.5g carbohydrate; 3.9g protein; 5.5g fibre

PICKLED ROOT VEGETABLE SALAD

with CASHEW CREAM

You will need to start this recipe the day before serving.

3 CUPS (750ML) WATER

2 CUPS (500ML) WHITE WINE VINEGAR

¼ CUP (50G) NORBU (MONK FRUIT SUGAR)

2 TABLESPOONS SEA SALT

400G (12½ OUNCES) BABY RAINBOW CARROTS, TRIMMED, SCRUBBED, HALVED LENGTHWAYS

1 MEDIUM KOHLRABI (400G), CUT INTO 1CM (½-INCH) THICK WEDGES

1 BABY FENNEL (130G), SLICED THINLY, FRONDS RESERVED

1 BUNCH BABY TURNIPS (130G), TRIMMED

8 SMALL RADISHES (120G), HALVED

1 TABLESPOON WHOLE MIXED PEPPERCORNS

1 TABLESPOON NIGELLA SEEDS

15G (½ OUNCE) MICRO RADISH LEAVES

CASHEW CREAM

300G (9½ OUNCES) SILKEN TOFU

¼ CUP (70G) CASHEW SPREAD

2 TEASPOONS FINELY GRATED LEMON RIND

1 SMALL CLOVE GARLIC, CRUSHED

1 Place the water and vinegar in a deep flat glass or ceramic dish; stir in norbu and salt until dissolved. Add vegetables, peppercorns, seeds and reserved fennel fronds, ensuring vegetables are covered (add extra water if necessary). Cover; refrigerate overnight.

2 Drain vegetables, reserving ¼ cup of the pickling liquid for the cashew cream.

3 Make cashew cream.

4 Serve pickled vegetables topped with cashew cream and micro leaves.

cashew cream Blend or process ingredients with reserved pickling liquid until smooth. Season to taste.

prep time 35 minutes (+ refrigeration) **serves** 4
nutritional count per serving 11.1g total fat (2g saturated fat); 1133kJ (271 cal); 20g carbohydrate; 15.9g protein; 13.1g fibre

tip Pickled vegetables can be made up to a week ahead; store, covered, in the refrigerator.

TO SHAVE FLESH FROM A FRESH COCONUT, WRAP THE COCONUT IN AN OLD, CLEAN TEA TOWEL THEN FIRMLY HIT THE COCONUT ON A HARD FLOOR (IDEALLY OUTSIDE, CLOSE TO A BOWL TO CATCH THE COCONUT WATER) TO BREAK THE HARD OUTER SHELL. SEPARATE AND DISCARD THE SHELL, THEN USE A PEELER TO SHAVE THE FLESH.

WARM INDIAN
BEAN SALAD

½ CUP (125ML) EXTRA VIRGIN OLIVE OIL

½ CUP (50G) SHAVED FRESH COCONUT (SEE TIP)

1 TEASPOON BROWN MUSTARD SEEDS

1 TEASPOON NIGELLA SEEDS

1 TEASPOON GARAM MASALA

2 SPRIGS CURRY LEAVES

250G (8 OUNCES) GREEN BEANS, TRIMMED

250G (8 OUNCES) FRESH ROMAN BEANS, TRIMMED, HALVED

¼ CUP (60ML) WATER

⅓ CUP (50G) ROASTED SALTED CASHEWS, CHOPPED COARSELY

1 FRESH LONG GREEN CHILLI, SLICED THINLY ON THE DIAGONAL

⅓ CUP (95G) GREEK-STYLE YOGHURT

ROTI AND LIME WEDGES, TO SERVE

1 Heat 2 tablespoons of the oil in a large frying pan over high heat, add coconut; cook, stirring occasionally, for 2 minutes or until golden brown. Drain on paper towel.

2 Heat remaining oil in same frying pan over high heat, add seeds, garam masala and curry leaves; cook, stirring, for 1 minute or until mustard seeds start to pop. Add beans; cook, stirring, for 2 minutes or until heated through and coated. Add the water; cook for a further 1 minute or until beans have softened slightly. Season to taste.

3 Add cashews, chilli and toasted coconut to bean mixture; toss gently to combine. Serve salad warm with yoghurt, roti and lime wedges.

prep + cook time 20 minutes **serves** 4 (as a side)
nutritional count per serving 40.5g total fat (9.5g saturated fat); 1836kJ (439 cal); 9.9g carbohydrate; 7g protein; 6.1g fibre

tip To make this a completely gluten-free meal, serve with your choice of gluten-free bread instead of roti.

KELP NOODLES ARE HIGH IN IODINE, GLUTEN-FREE AND LOW CARB, THEY CAN BE FOUND IN HEALTH FOOD STORES AND SOME ASIAN SUPERMARKETS. YOU CAN USE MUNG BEAN THREAD NOODLES OR GLASS RICE VERMICELLI NOODLES INSTEAD.

ASIAN KELP NOODLE And HERB SALAD

454G (14½ OUNCES) KELP NOODLES

¼ CUP (35G) ROASTED UNSALTED CASHEWS, CHOPPED FINELY

¼ CUP (35G) ROASTED UNSALTED PEANUTS, CHOPPED FINELY

½ CUP LOOSELY PACKED FRESH MINT LEAVES

½ CUP LOOSELY PACKED FRESH CORIANDER (CILANTRO) LEAVES

½ CUP LOOSELY PACKED FRESH THAI BASIL LEAVES

2 TABLESPOONS COARSELY CHOPPED VIETNAMESE MINT

1 GREEN ONION (SCALLION), SLICED THINLY

GARLIC & LIME DRESSING

2 TABLESPOONS HOT WATER

1 SMALL CLOVE GARLIC, CRUSHED

1½ TABLESPOONS FISH SAUCE

1½ TABLESPOONS LIME JUICE

1 FRESH LONG RED CHILLI, SEEDED, CHOPPED FINELY

1½ TABLESPOONS COCONUT SUGAR

1 Soak noodles in a large heatproof bowl of boiling water for 10 minutes or until tender; drain.

2 Meanwhile, make garlic and lime dressing.

3 Return noodles to bowl with remaining ingredients; toss gently to combine. Drizzle salad with dressing; serve immediately.

garlic & lime dressing Place ingredients in a screw-top jar; shake well. Season to taste.

prep + cook time 15 minutes **serves** 4 (as a side)

nutritional count per serving 8.6g total fat (1.3g saturated fat); 621kJ (148 cal); 11.2g carbohydrate; 5g protein; 3.6g fibre

serving suggestion Add some coarsely shredded cooked chicken, prawns or tofu to make this a protein packed main meal.

COOKING EGGPLANT IN A FRYING PAN REQUIRES A SUBSTANTIAL AMOUNT OF OIL. STEAMING THE EGGPLANT BEFORE FRYING, REDUCES THE AMOUNT OF OIL YOU NEED, MAKING IT A HEALTHIER OPTION.

MISO EGGPLANT
 GINGER SALAD

8 BABY EGGPLANT (480G), HALVED LENGTHWAYS

¼ CUP (60G) MISO PASTE

¼ CUP (60ML) MIRIN

2 TEASPOONS FINELY GRATED FRESH GINGER

2 TEASPOONS HONEY

¼ CUP (60ML) OLIVE OIL

1 TABLESPOON DRAINED PICKLED GINGER

1 GREEN ONION (SCALLION), SLICED THINLY ON THE DIAGONAL

3 TEASPOONS SESAME SEEDS, TOASTED

1 Steam eggplant, covered, over a large saucepan of simmering water for 7 minutes or until tender.

2 Meanwhile, whisk miso, mirin, fresh ginger and honey in a small bowl until combined.

3 Heat oil in a large frying pan over high heat. Coat eggplant in miso mixture; cook eggplant, in two batches, for 1 minute on each side or until browned. Remove from pan; wipe pan clean with paper towel between batches.

4 Serve eggplant topped with pickled ginger, green onion and sesame seeds.

prep + cook time 20 minutes **serves** 4 (as a side)
nutritional count per serving 16.1g total fat (2.4g saturated fat); 983kJ (235 cal); 17.5g carbohydrate; 3.5g protein; 4.2g fibre
serving suggestion Serve with steamed fish and asian greens.

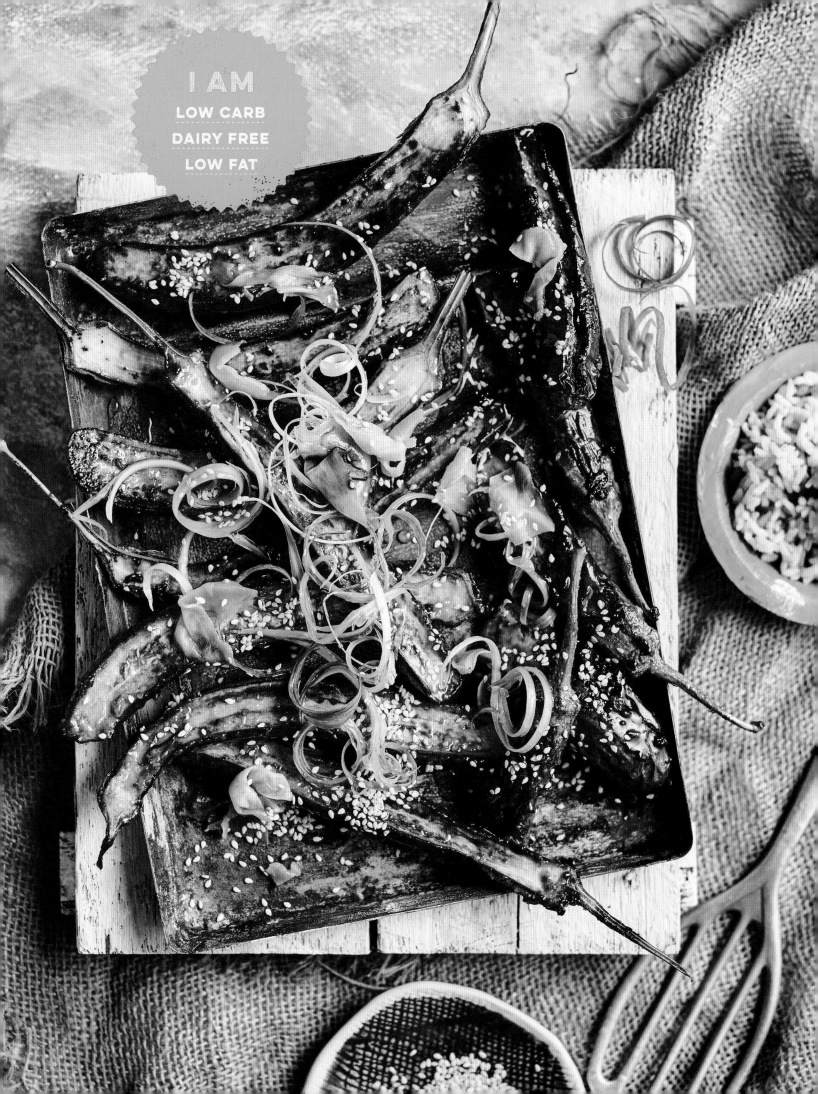

I AM

LOW FAT

VEGETARIAN

RAW

A SPIRALIZER IS A KITCHEN GADGET THAT CUTS VEGETABLES TO RESEMBLE NOODLES. IF YOU DON'T HAVE ONE, YOU CAN COARSELY GRATE THE VEGETABLES OR USE A MANDOLINE OR V-SLICER. THIS SALAD IS PERFECT SERVED AT A BARBECUE. SALAD CAN BE EASILY DOUBLED OR TRIPLED TO SERVE A CROWD.

RAW VEGETABLE
NOODLE SALAD

2 MEDIUM ZUCCHINI (240G)

2 MEDIUM CARROTS (240G)

2 MEDIUM PURPLE CARROTS (240G)

½ SMALL DAIKON (200G)

½ CUP FIRMLY PACKED FRESH FLAT-LEAF PARSLEY LEAVES

2 TABLESPOONS FINELY CHOPPED FRESH CHIVES

CREAMY MUSTARD DRESSING

½ CUP (140G) GREEK-STYLE YOGHURT

2 TABLESPOONS WHOLEGRAIN MUSTARD

2 TABLESPOONS EXTRA VIRGIN OLIVE OIL

1 TABLESPOON LEMON JUICE

1 Make creamy mustard dressing.

2 Using a vegetable spiralizer, cut zucchini, carrots and daikon into thick noodles.

3 Place vegetable 'noodles' in a large bowl with herbs and dressing; toss gently to combine.

creamy mustard dressing Whisk ingredients in a medium bowl until combined; season to taste.

prep + cook time 15 minutes **serves** 6 (as a side)

nutritional count per serving 8g total fat (1.8g saturated fat); 553kJ (132 cal); 9.5g carbohydrate; 3g protein; 5.2g fibre

BROCCOLI STEAKS
with QUINOA And RICOTTA

½ CUP (100G) WHITE QUINOA

700G (1½ POUNDS) BROCCOLI, CUT INTO 1CM (½-INCH) THICK SLICES

2 SMALL ZUCCHINI (180G), SLICED THINLY

1 TABLESPOON OLIVE OIL

80G (2½ OUNCES) RICOTTA, CRUMBLED

2 TABLESPOONS NATURAL FLAKED ALMONDS

2 TABLESPOONS DRIED UNSWEETENED CRANBERRIES

LEMON DRESSING

¼ CUP (60ML) EXTRA VIRGIN OLIVE OIL

2 TABLESPOONS LEMON JUICE

1 TEASPOON FINELY GRATED LEMON RIND

1 SMALL CLOVE GARLIC, CRUSHED

1 Preheat oven to 180°C/350°F.

2 Rinse quinoa under cold water; drain well. Spread on an oven tray. Bake for 10 minutes, stirring halfway through, or until toasted and golden. Cool.

3 Combine broccoli, zucchini and oil in a large bowl until vegetables are coated. Cook broccoli on a heated oiled grill plate (or grill or barbecue) over medium-high heat for 3 minutes, each side or until just cooked. Remove from heat; cover to keep warm. Cook zucchini on heated oiled grill plate for 1 minute each side.

4 Make lemon dressing.

5 Arrange vegetables on a serving platter, top with ricotta, quinoa, almonds and cranberries. Serve drizzled with dressing.

lemon dressing Whisk ingredients in a small bowl; season to taste.

prep + cook time 20 minutes **serves** 4

nutritional count per serving 26.3g total fat (4.8g saturated fat); 1677kJ (400 cal); 22.2g carbohydrate; 14.9g protein; 9.4g fibre

tip Add a pinch of crushed chilli flakes to the quinoa for the final minute of baking time.

I AM

EGG FREE

VEGETARIAN

LOW FAT

I AM

EGG FREE

HIGH IN FOLATE

LOW FAT

THE CELERY HEART IS THE PALE AND LESS FIBROUS INNER SECTION OF THE BUNCH. KEEP ANY LEFTOVER OUTER STALKS FOR VEGIE STICKS OR STOCK. USE A MANDOLINE OR V-SLICER TO SHAVE THE VEGETABLES INTO VERY THIN SLICES.

BARLEY *And* BRUSSELS SPROUT
WALDORF SALAD

¾ CUP (150G) PEARL BARLEY

2½ CUPS (625ML) WATER

200G (6½ OUNCES) BRUSSEL SPROUTS, SHAVED

1 CELERY HEART (235G), SHAVED, PLUS ¼ CUP PALE GREEN LEAVES

3 BABY RED-SKINNED APPLES (195G), SLICED THINLY

3 BABY CORRELLA PEARS (165G), SLICED THINLY

⅓ CUP (35G) WALNUT HALVES, ROASTED

¼ CUP FRESH DILL SPRIGS

BUTTERMILK YOGHURT DRESSING

⅓ CUP (80ML) BUTTERMILK

¼ CUP (70G) GREEK-STYLE YOGHURT

1 TABLESPOON CHOPPED FRESH DILL

1 TABLESPOON CIDER VINEGAR OR LEMON JUICE

½ SMALL CLOVE GARLIC, CRUSHED

1 Place barley and the water in a medium saucepan with a pinch of salt; bring to the boil. Reduce heat to low; simmer, covered, for 30 minutes, or until liquid has been absorbed and grains are tender. Drain; rinse under cold running water.

2 Meanwhile, make buttermilk yoghurt dressing.

3 Place barley in a medium bowl with sprouts, shaved celery, apple and pear; toss gently to combine. Drizzle salad with dressing; top with walnuts, celery leaves and dill sprigs.

buttermilk yoghurt dressing Whisk ingredients in a small bowl; season to taste.

prep + cook time 45 minutes **serves** 4

nutritional count per serving 9g total fat (1.6g saturated fat); 1333kJ (319 cal); 42.8g carbohydrate; 9.8g protein; 13.4g fibre

serving suggestion Add 200g (6½ ounces) flaked hot smoked trout or serve with pan-fried salmon fillets.

THERE ARE TWO TYPES OF PERSIMMONS: A SOFT, ASTRINGENT ONE AND A FIRM, NON-ASTRINGENT SWEET VARIETY ALSO KNOWN AS FUJI FRUIT. WE USED THE SWEET VARIETY IN THIS RECIPE. WHEN PERSIMMONS ARE OUT OF SEASON, USE PEARS INSTEAD.

CHAR-GRILLED PERSIMMONS

AVOCADO And WATERCRESS SALAD

2 MEDIUM PERSIMMONS (FUJI) (860G), SLICED THICKLY

2 TABLESPOONS OLIVE OIL

1 LARGE AVOCADO (320G), CHOPPED

2 CUPS (60G) PICKED WATERCRESS SPRIGS

¼ CUP (35G) SUNFLOWER SEED KERNELS, TOASTED

BUTTERMILK DRESSING

⅓ CUP (80ML) BUTTERMILK

1 TEASPOON HONEY

2 TEASPOONS CHOPPED FRESH TARRAGON

½ CLOVE GARLIC, CRUSHED

1 Make buttermilk dressing.

2 Toss persimmons in olive oil to coat; season.

3 Cook persimmons, on a heated oiled grill plate (or grill or barbecue) over high heat for 1 minute each side or until grill marks appear.

4 Arrange avocado, persimmon and watercress on a large platter; sprinkle with sunflower seeds and drizzle with dressing. Season. Serve immediately.

buttermilk dressing Place ingredients in a screw-top jar; shake well. Season to taste.

prep + cook time 20 minutes (+ standing)

serves 4 (as a side)

nutritional count per serving 26.4g total fat (4.7g saturated fat); 1772kJ (432 cal); 38.4g carbohydrate; 5.7g protein; 8.6g fibre

I AM

HIGH FIBRE

HIGH IN VITAMIN C

EGG FREE

I AM
HIGH FIBRE
PROTEIN RICH
LOW FAT

SPICY PUMPKIN & CAULIFLOWER

With YOGHURT DRESSING

750G (1½ POUNDS) JAP PUMPKIN, PEELED, CUT INTO 2CM (¾-INCH) THICK WEDGES

750G (1½ POUNDS) CAULIFLOWER, CUT INTO FLORETS

1 TABLESPOON OLIVE OIL

2 TEASPOONS GROUND CORIANDER

2 TEASPOONS GROUND CUMIN

½ TEASPOON GROUND CINNAMON

½ CUP (100G) BROWN RICE

2 LITRES (8 CUPS) WATER

2 TABLESPOONS SLICED DRAINED PICKLED JALAPEÑOS

1 TABLESPOON SUNFLOWER SEED KERNELS OR PEPITAS (PUMPKIN SEED KERNELS)

MICRO HERBS, TO SERVE

YOGHURT DRESSING

1 CUP (280G) LOW-FAT GREEK-STYLE YOGHURT

2 TABLESPOONS FINELY CHOPPED DRAINED PICKLED JALAPEÑOS

2 TABLESPOONS COARSELY CHOPPED FRESH CORIANDER (CILANTRO)

1 TEASPOON FINELY GRATED LEMON RIND

1 TABLESPOON LEMON JUICE

1 Preheat oven to 200°C/400°F.

2 Combine pumpkin, cauliflower, oil and spices on a large oven tray until vegetables are well coated; spread evenly, in a single layer. Season. Roast for 30 minutes or until cauliflower is tender.

3 Meanwhile, place rice and the water in a medium saucepan; bring to the boil. Boil for 30 minutes or until rice is tender. Drain well.

4 Make yoghurt dressing.

5 Spoon rice onto a large serving platter; top with roasted vegetables. Drizzle with dressing; sprinkle with jalapeños, seeds and micro herbs.

yoghurt dressing Stir ingredients in a medium bowl until combined.

prep + cook time 45 minutes serves 4

nutritional count per serving 11.9g total fat (3.4g saturated fat); 1635kJ (390 cal); 51.5g carbohydrate; 13g protein; 12g fibre

serving suggestion Serve with roast lamb or barbecued lamb leg steaks.

TO SAVE TIME, USE 400G (12½ OUNCES) CANNED DRAINED LENTILS AND 400G (12½ OUNCES) CANNED QUALITY RED SALMON.

SALMON *And* GREEN LENTIL
NISCOISE SALAD

¾ CUP (150G) DRIED FRENCH-STYLE
GREEN LENTILS, RINSED

½ MEDIUM WHITE ONION (75G), HALVED

1 BAY LEAF

3 SMALL KUMARA (ORANGE SWEET POTATO)
(250G), CUT INTO 5MM (¼-INCH) ROUND SLICES

OLIVE OIL COOKING SPRAY

4 X 100G (3-OUNCE) SALMON FILLETS, SKIN ON

4 FREE-RANGE EGGS

200G (6½ OUNCES) GREEN BEANS, TRIMMED

1 SMALL RADICCHIO (150G), LEAVES SEPARATED

OLIVE DRESSING

¼ CUP (60ML) EXTRA VIRGIN OLIVE OIL

2 TABLESPOONS FINELY CHOPPED
KALAMATA OLIVES

2 TABLESPOONS FINELY CHOPPED RED ONION

1½ TABLESPOONS RED WINE VINEGAR

2 TEASPOONS WHOLEGRAIN MUSTARD

2 TEASPOONS PURE MAPLE SYRUP

1 Preheat oven to 200°C/400°F.

2 Bring a medium saucepan of salted water to the boil. Add lentils, onion and bay leaf; reduce heat to low, simmer, uncovered, for 20 minutes or until just tender. Drain well. Remove and discard onion and bay leaf.

3 Meanwhile, place kumara, in a single layer, over two-thirds of a baking-paper-lined oven tray; spray with oil, season. Bake for 10 minutes. Add salmon to tray; spray with oil, season. Bake a further 7 minutes or until salmon and kumara are just cooked through. Remove from tray.

4 Place eggs in a medium saucepan with enough cold water to cover; bring to boil. Reduce heat; simmer, uncovered, for 4 minutes for soft boiled, adding beans for the final minute of cooking. Drain; refresh eggs and beans under cold running water. Peel eggs.

5 Make olive dressing.

6 Divide lentils and radicchio among serving plates; drizzle with half the dressing. Top with beans, kumara, salmon and halved eggs; drizzle with remaining dressing.

olive dressing Place ingredients in a screw-top jar; shake well. Season to taste.

prep + cook time 35 minutes **serves** 4
nutritional count per serving 33.9g total fat (7.4g saturated fat); 2670kJ (638 cal); 31.6g carbohydrate; 47.9g protein; 9.5g fibre

I AM
PROTEIN RICH
HIGH IN OMEGA 3
NUT FREE

DRESSINGS

GREEN OLIVE

prep time 10 minutes **makes** 1 cup

Place 1 cup drained pitted green olives, ¼ cup chopped fresh flat-leaf parsley, 2 tablespoons lemon juice, 1 tablespoon drained capers, ⅓ cup extra virgin olive oil and 1 clove crushed garlic in a small food processor; process to combine. Thin down with a little extra oil, if necessary.

tip Serve with char-grilled vegetables.

CREAMY DUKKAH

prep time 10 minutes **makes** 1 cup

Whisk 1 tablespoon extra virgin olive oil, 1 crushed clove garlic, 2 tablespoons lemon juice, 1 teaspoon honey, ½ cup greek-style yoghurt and 2 tablespoons pistachio dukkah in a jug intil combined.

tip Serve with char-grilled lamb or chicken.

ROASTED CAPSICUM

prep time 10 minutes **makes** 1¼ cups

Place 200g (6½oz) drained bottled roasted capsicums (bell pepper), 2 tablespoons lime juice, ½ teaspoon mexican chilli powder, 1 clove crushed garlic, ¼ cup coarsely chopped fresh coriander (cilantro) and ¼ cup olive oil in a small food processor; process to combine.
tip Serve with sliced char-grilled chicken and pasta or make without the lime juice and use as a sauce base for pizza.

JAPANESE DRESSING

prep time 10 minutes **makes** ⅓ cup

Stir 2 tablespoons japanese soy sauce, 2 tablespoons rice vinegar, 1 tablespoon mirin, ½ teaspoon sesame oil, 1 finely chopped green onion (scallion), 1 teaspoon drained shredded pickled ginger and 2 teaspoons toasted sesame seeds in a bowl until combined.
tip Serve with steamed asian greens or cooked flaked salmon tossed with soba noodles.

I AM
HIGH FIBRE
PROTEIN RICH
NUT FREE

WILD RICE IS A LONG DARK BROWN GRAIN WHICH HAS A NUTTY TEXTURE AND HOLDS ITS SHAPE WELL DURING COOKING. CHICKEN SUPREME IS CHICKEN BREAST FILLETS WITH SKIN ON, AVAILABLE FROM BUTCHER SHOPS AND CHICKEN SHOPS.

WILD RICE
CHICKEN *And* MUSHROOM SALAD

¾ CUP (150G) WILD RICE

2 TEASPOONS HONEY

1 TABLESPOON FRESH THYME LEAVES

1 MEDIUM ORANGE (240G)

1 CLOVE GARLIC, CRUSHED

2 TABLESPOONS OLIVE OIL

2 SMALL CHICKEN BREAST SUPREME (SKIN ON) (500G) (SEE TIPS)

400G (12½ OUNCES) PORTOBELLO MUSHROOMS

350G (11 OUNCES) WATERCRESS, LEAVES PICKED

1 MEDIUM RED ONION (170G), SLICED THINLY

FIG DRESSING

3 DRIED FIGS (50G), SLICED THINLY

½ CUP (125ML) FRESHLY SQUEEZED ORANGE JUICE

1 TABLESPOON RED WINE VINEGAR

1 Preheat oven to 180°C/350°F.

2 Place rice in a medium saucepan with enough cold water to cover; bring to the boil. Reduce heat to medium; simmer for 30 minutes or until tender. Drain well; rinse under cold water.

3 Meanwhile, finely grate rind from the orange. Cut the top and bottom from the orange; cut off the white pith, following the curve of the fruit. Cut down both sides of the white membrane to release each segment.

4 Combine grated rind, honey, thyme, garlic and half the oil in a large bowl; add chicken, toss to coat in marinade. Toss mushrooms in remaining oil; season. Arrange chicken mixture and mushrooms on an oven tray. Roast for 25 minutes or until just cooked through. Remove chicken; rest, covered, for 5 minutes. Slice thinly.

5 Make fig dressing.

6 Combine rice with half the dressing; top with chicken, mushrooms, watercress, onion and orange segments. Serve drizzled with remaining dressing.

fig dressing Place figs and juice in a small saucepan; bring to the boil. Reduce heat to low; simmer, covered, for 5 minutes. Stir in vinegar; cool.

prep + cook time 50 minutes **serves** 4

nutritional count per serving 20.8g total fat (4.7g saturated fat); 2238kJ (534 cal); 51.7g carbohydrate; 30.2g protein; 10.3g fibre

KALE CAESAR SALAD

with CHICKPEA CROÛTONS

4 FREE-RANGE EGGS

500G (1 POUND) KALE, TRIMMED, CHOPPED COARSELY

1 TABLESPOON OLIVE OIL

½ TEASPOON SEA SALT

½ CUP (40G) SHAVED PARMESAN

MICRO RADISH LEAVES, TO SERVE

CHICKPEA CROÛTONS

400G (12½ OUNCES) CANNED CHICKPEAS (GARBANZO BEANS), DRAINED, RINSED

1 TABLESPOON OLIVE OIL

1 TEASPOON SMOKED PAPRIKA

¼ CUP (40G) SMOKED ALMONDS, CHOPPED

BUTTERMILK DRESSING

⅓ CUP (80ML) BUTTERMILK

2 TEASPOONS LEMON JUICE

1 TEASPOON DIJON MUSTARD

1 LARGE ANCHOVY FILLET, CHOPPED FINELY

½ CLOVE GARLIC, CRUSHED

1 Make chickpea croûtons.

2 Meanwhile, place eggs in a medium saucepan with enough cold water to cover; bring to the boil. Reduce heat; simmer, uncovered, for 4 minutes for soft boiled. Drain; refresh under cold running water. Peel eggs.

3 Make buttermilk dressing.

4 Place kale, oil and salt in a large bowl; rub well to soften the leaves, it will lose about half its volume. Add chickpea croûtons and half the dressing; toss gently to combine. Serve topped with halved eggs, parmesan, micro leaves and remaining dressing.

chickpea croûtons Combine ingredients in a medium bowl. Cook chickpea mixture in a large frying pan over high heat, stirring, for 8 minutes, or until crisp. Cool.

buttermilk dressing Place ingredients in a screw-top jar; shake well.

prep + cook time 20 minutes **serves** 4

nutritional count per serving 24.9g total fat (6g saturated fat); 1547kJ (369 cal); 13.9g carbohydrate; 19.8g protein; 7g fibre

tip You could use baby kale leaves if you prefer, as they are not as tough as regular kale.

serving suggestion Add some sliced smoked chicken.

I AM
VITAMIN A
HIGH IN IRON
LOW GI

I AM

LOW CARB

VEGETARIAN

EGG FREE

SUPER GREEN SALAD

with GREEN GODDESS DRESSING

¾ CUP (25G) PUFFED MILLET

⅓ CUP (45G) SHELLED PISTACHIOS, CHOPPED COARSELY

175G (5½ OUNCES) BROCCOLINI, TRIMMED, SLICED LENGTHWAYS

200G (6½ OUNCES) SNOW PEAS, TRIMMED

1 LEBANESE CUCUMBER (130G), SLICED LENGTHWAYS

1 MEDIUM AVOCADO (250G), SLICED

⅔ CUP (70G) MIXED CRUNCHY SPROUTS

⅔ CUP (30G) ALFALFA SPROUTS

GREEN GODDESS DRESSING

¼ CUP (70G) GREEK-STYLE YOGHURT

¼ CUP (60G) SOUR CREAM

1 SMALL CLOVE GARLIC, CRUSHED

¼ CUP COARSELY CHOPPED FRESH FLAT-LEAF PARSLEY

¼ CUP COARSELY CHOPPED FRESH CHIVES

1 TABLESPOON CHOPPED FRESH TARRAGON

1 TABLESPOON LEMON JUICE

1 Preheat oven to 180°C/350°F.

2 Spread millet and pistachios on an oven tray. Bake for 5 minutes, stirring halfway through cooking, or until millet is crisp. Cool on tray.

3 Meanwhile, place broccolini and sugar snap peas in a colander in the sink. Bring a jug of water to the boil. Pour boiling water over vegetables to lightly blanch. Rinse under cold water; drain well.

4 Make green goddess dressing.

5 Arrange broccolini and snow peas with cucumber and avocado on a serving platter; top with millet mixture and sprouts. Serve drizzled with dressing.

green goddess dressing Blend ingredients in a blender until smooth. Season to taste.

prep + cook time 20 minutes **serves** 4
nutritional count per serving 22.7g total fat (7.2g saturated fat); 1273kJ (304 cal); 12g carbohydrate; 9.6g protein; 7.1g fibre
tip Salad is best assembled close to serving.

MOUNTAIN RICE BLEND IS A COMBINATION OF BROWN RICE, BLACK RICE AND RED RICE. YOU CAN USE FROZEN PEAS INSTEAD OF BROAD BEANS, IF YOU LIKE.

MOUNTAIN RICE
SALAD with HALOUMI

¼ CUP (60ML) RED WINE VINEGAR

1 TABLESPOON DIJON MUSTARD

¼ CUP (60ML) OLIVE OIL

¼ CUP (90G) HONEY

1 CUP (200G) MOUNTAIN RICE BLEND

500G (1 POUND) FROZEN BROAD (FAVA) BEANS, BLANCHED, PEELED

1 BABY FENNEL (130G), TRIMMED, SLICED THINLY

400G (12½ OUNCES) HEIRLOOM TOMATOES, CUT INTO WEDGES

100G (3 OUNCES) CHAMPAGNE RADISHES, SLICED THINLY

½ CUP COARSELY CHOPPED FRESH DILL

250G (8 OUNCES) HALOUMI CHEESE, CUT INTO 1CM (½-INCH) SLICES

1 Place vinegar, mustard, 2 tablespoons of the oil and 2 tablespoons of the honey in a screw-top jar; shake well.

2 Cook rice in a large saucepan of boiling water for 20 minutes or until tender. Drain; rinse well. Transfer to a large bowl with half the dressing; mix well.

3 Add broad beans, fennel, tomatoes, radishes and half the dill to rice; toss to combine.

4 Heat remaining oil in a large non-stick frying pan over medium-high heat; cook haloumi for 3 minutes on each side or until golden brown. Drizzle with the remaining honey.

5 Serve rice salad on a large platter, topped with haloumi and honey juices; drizzle with remaining dressing and top with remaining dill.

prep + cook time 50 minutes **serves** 4
nutritional count per serving 26.2g total fat (9.2g saturated fat); 2555kJ (610 cal); 62.5g carbohydrate; 25.3g protein; 10.9g fibre

I AM
PROTEIN RICH
HIGH IN VITAMIN C
GLUTEN FREE

KIMCHI 2 WAYS

CHEAT'S KIMCHI

1.5 LITRES (6 CUPS) WARM WATER

1 CUP (250G) COOKING SALT

450G (14½ OUNCES) WOMBOK (NAPA CABBAGE), CUT LENGTHWAYS INTO WEDGES, CORE INTACT

4 GREEN ONIONS (SCALLIONS), CUT INTO 10CM (4-INCH) LENGTHS

½ CUP (125ML) RICE WINE VINEGAR

2 TABLESPOONS RICE MALT SYRUP

1 TEASPOON SESAME OIL

1 TABLESPOON KOREAN CHILLI PASTE (GOCHUJANG)

1 FRESH LONG RED CHILLI, SEEDED, HALVED LENGTHWAYS

1 Combine the water and salt in a large bowl. Add wombok and green onion; stand for 1 hour or until wombok leaves have softened. Drain. Rinse very well under cold running water to remove most of the brine; pat dry.

2 Whisk vinegar, syrup, oil and chilli paste in a medium bowl until combined.

3 Place wombok, green onion and chilli in a 3 cup (750ml) sterilised jar; pour in vinegar mixture to cover. Refrigerate overnight before serving.

prep time 45 minutes (+ standing & refrigeration)

makes 3 cups

nutritional count per ½ cup 1.1g total fat (0.1g saturated fat); 243kJ (58 cal); 9g carbohydrate; 2.4g protein; 2.5g fibre

tips For information on sterilising jars, see page 236. Store bottled kimchi in the fridge for up to 2 weeks.

RED CABBAGE KIMCHI

1.5 LITRES (6 CUPS) WARM WATER

1 CUP (250G) COOKING SALT

450G (14½ OUNCES) RED CABBAGE, CUT INTO 4 WEDGES

1 SMALL CARROT (70G), SLICED THINLY LENGTHWAYS

4 GREEN ONIONS (SCALLIONS), CUT INTO 10CM (4-INCH) LENGTHS

½ CUP (125ML) RICE WINE VINEGAR

2 TABLESPOONS RICE MALT SYRUP

1 TEASPOON SESAME OIL

1 TABLESPOON KOREAN CHILLI PASTE (GOCHUJANG)

1 Combine the water and salt in a large bowl. Add cabbage, carrot and green onion; stand for 1 hour or until cabbage leaves have softened. Drain. Rinse very well under cold running water to remove most of the brine; pat dry.

2 Whisk vinegar, syrup, oil and chilli paste in a medium bowl until combined.

3 Layer cabbage, carrot and green onion in a 3 cup (750ml) sterilised jar; pour in vinegar mixture to cover. Refrigerate overnight before serving.

prep time 45 minutes (+ standing & refrigeration)

makes 3 cups

nutritional count per ½ cup 1.2g total fat (0.2g saturated fat); 286kJ (69 cal); 11g carbohydrate; 2.2g protein; 3.5g fibre

tips For information on sterilising jars, see page 236. Store bottled kimchi in the fridge for up to 2 weeks.

SUPER MAINS

BUSY FAMILY LIFE MEANS IT'S ALL TOO EASY TO OPT FOR FAST AND CONVENIENT TO FILL HUNGRY BELLIES. BUT IT IS POSSIBLE TO MAKE YOUR OWN QUICK 'SUPER' MEALS WITH THESE RECIPES THAT EVEN THE KIDS WILL LOVE.

INSTEAD OF FRESH CORN, YOU CAN COOK
1½ CUPS (240G) FROZEN CORN KERNELS UNTIL JUST TENDER.
PORTERHOUSE OR SIRLOIN STEAK CAN ALSO BE USED.

MEXICAN
BEEF And CORN SALAD

2 CORN COBS (800G), TRIMMED,
HUSK AND SILKS REMOVED

2 TABLESPOONS OLIVE OIL

2 TABLESPOONS LIME JUICE

500G (1 POUND) BEEF RUMP STEAKS, TRIMMED

2 TEASPOONS GROUND CUMIN

1 TEASPOON SMOKED PAPRIKA

PINCH CAYENNE PEPPER

8 X 20CM (8-INCH) WHOLEGRAIN TORTILLAS

420G (13½ OUNCES) CANNED KIDNEY BEANS,
DRAINED, RINSED

200G (6½ OUNCES) BABY ROMA (EGG)
TOMATOES, HALVED

1 MEDIUM AVOCADO (250G), SLICED

½ CUP COARSELY CHOPPED FRESH
CORIANDER (CILANTRO) LEAVES

PEPITA SAUCE

¼ CUP (50G) PEPITAS (PUMPKIN SEED KERNELS)

½ CUP FRESH CORIANDER (CILANTRO) LEAVES

1 CLOVE GARLIC, CRUSHED

2 TABLESPOONS OLIVE OIL

2 TABLESPOONS LIME JUICE

¼ CUP (70G) GREEK-STYLE YOGHURT

1 Place each corn cob on a sheet of foil; brush cobs with 2 teaspoons of the oil and half the juice. Wrap foil tightly around each cob. Cook corn on heated oiled grill plate (or grill or barbecue) over medium heat, turning occasionally, for 15 minutes or until tender. Cool for 10 minutes. When cool enough to handle, cut kernels from corn.

2 Make pepita sauce.

3 Brush steaks with 2 teaspoons of the remaining oil; sprinkle with spices. Season. Cook steaks on heated oiled grill plate over medium-high heat, for 3 minutes each side, for medium-rare or until cooked as desired. Remove from heat; rest, covered with foil, for 5 minutes.

4 Meanwhile, place tortillas on heated grill plate for 30 seconds each side until charred lightly.

5 Place corn kernels in a large bowl with beans, tomatoes, avocado, coriander, remaining oil and remaining juice; toss gently to combine. Season.

6 Cut steak into thin slices. Top each tortilla with corn salad and sliced steak; serve drizzled with sauce.

pepita sauce Process pepitas, coriander, garlic and oil in a food processor until well combined. Add juice and yoghurt; process until smooth. Season to taste.

prep + cook time 45 minutes serves 4

nutritional count per serving 49.9g total fat (11.6g saturated fat); 3970kJ (948 cal); 55g carbohydrate; 61g protein; 16.9g fibre

I AM

HIGH FIBRE
PROTEIN RICH
LOW GI

I AM
PROTEIN RICH
HIGH IN OMEGA 3
POTASSIUM

YOU WILL NEED ABOUT 5 TABLESPOONS OF DUKKAH.
SALAD CAN BE DRESSED UP TO 30 MINUTES BEFORE SERVING.

SALMON PATTIES
WITH ZUCCHINI And ASPARAGUS SALAD

2 X 200G (6½-OUNCE) SKINLESS SALMON FILLETS, HALVED CROSSWAYS

2 GREEN ONIONS (SCALLIONS), TRIMMED, SLICED THINLY, RESERVE TRIMMINGS

5CM (2-INCH) STRIP LEMON RIND

4 WHOLE BLACK PEPPERCORNS

1 CUP (250ML) WATER

¾ CUP (150G) COUSCOUS

1 TABLESPOON OLIVE OIL

¼ CUP COARSELY CHOPPED FRESH FLAT-LEAF PARSLEY

2 FREE-RANGE EGGS, BEATEN LIGHTLY

45G (1½-OUNCE) PACKET LEMON AND HERB DUKKAH, PLUS EXTRA TO SERVE

⅓ CUP (80ML) OLIVE OIL, EXTRA

1 MEDIUM ZUCCHINI (120G)

170G (5½ OUNCES) ASPARAGUS, TRIMMED

½ TEASPOON FINELY GRATED LEMON RIND

1 TABLESPOON LEMON JUICE

⅔ CUP (190G) GREEK-STYLE YOGHURT

1 Place salmon, reserved green onion trimmings, rind, peppercorns and the water in a medium saucepan; bring to the boil. Remove from heat; stand for 10 minutes. Remove salmon from poaching liquid to a plate; remove and discard green onion, rind and peppercorns.

2 Bring poaching liquid back to the boil. Remove from heat; stir in couscous. Stand; covered for 5 minutes or until liquid is absorbed. Separate grains with a fork.

3 Place couscous in a medium bowl with oil; mix well. Add flaked salmon, green onion, parsley and half the egg; season. With wet hands, shape mixture into eight patties; place on a baking-paper-lined oven tray.

4 Place remaining egg and dukkah in separate small bowls. Dip patties in egg, draining off excess; coat in dukkah.

5 Heat half the extra oil in a large frying pan over medium heat; cook patties, in two batches, for 3 minutes each side or until golden and heated through. Drain on paper towel.

6 Use a mandoline or V-slicer to thinly slice zucchini and asparagus into ribbons. Place in a medium bowl with combined rind, juice and remaining extra oil; toss gently.

7 Serve patties with salad, yoghurt and extra dukkah.

prep + cook time 40 minutes **serves** 4

nutritional count per serving 40.3g total fat (8.5g saturated fat); 2716kJ (649 cal); 37.3g carbohydrate; 32.8g protein; 2.9g fibre

TOMATO, CARROT AND CUCUMBER CAN ALSO BE USED IN THIS RECIPE.
THE COOKED MINCE CAN BE FROZEN FOR UP TO 3 MONTHS.
IF YOU DON'T HAVE COCONUT OIL USE OLIVE OIL INSTEAD.

TURKEY
'LARB' LETTUCE CUPS

1 TABLESPOON JASMINE RICE

1 TABLESPOON COCONUT OIL

3 CLOVES GARLIC, CHOPPED

1 LEMON GRASS STALK, WHITE PART ONLY, SLICED THINLY

3 KAFFIR LIME LEAVES, SHREDDED

500G (1 POUND) MINCED (GROUND) TURKEY

1 SMALL FENNEL (130G), SLICED THINLY

8 BUTTER (BOSTON) LETTUCE LEAVES

1 FRESH LONG GREEN CHILLI, SLICED THINLY

½ CUP MICRO RADISH LEAVES

½ CUP SMALL FRESH MINT LEAVES

VIETNAMESE DRESSING

¼ CUP (60ML) FISH SAUCE

¼ CUP (60ML) LIME JUICE

2 TABLESPOONS FINELY GRATED PALM SUGAR

1 Make vietnamese dressing.

2 Cook rice in a small frying pan over medium-high heat, stirring, for 3 minutes or until lightly toasted. Pound rice in a mortar and pestle until coarsely crushed.

3 Heat coconut oil in a large non-stick frying pan over medium heat, add garlic, lemon grass and lime leaves; cook, stirring, for 30 seconds or until fragrant.

4 Increase heat to high, add turkey; cook, stirring to break up lumps, for 7 minutes or until cooked. Add half the dressing; cook, stirring, for 1 minute.

5 Spoon turkey mixture and fennel into lettuce leaves; top with chilli, herbs and crushed rice. Serve lettuce cups with remaining dressing.

vietnamese dressing Stir ingredients in a small bowl until sugar dissolves.

prep + cook time 30 minutes (+ cooling) **serves** 4
nutritional count per serving 9g total fat (5.4g saturated fat); 1061kJ (253 cal); 11.7g carbohydrate; 29.6g protein; 2.5g fibre
serving suggestion Serve with steamed rice.

I AM

LOW CARB

PROTEIN RICH

LOW FAT

BUCKWHEAT SOBA NOODLES
WITH MISO SALMON

270G (8½ OUNCES) BUCKWHEAT SOBA NOODLES

1 TABLESPOON MISO PASTE (LIGHT)

1 TABLESPOON RICE WINE VINEGAR

1 TABLESPOON RICE MALT SYRUP

1 TABLESPOON VEGETABLE OIL

2 X 280G (9-OUNCE) SALMON FILLETS, SKIN REMOVED

8 GREEN ONIONS (SCALLIONS), TRIMMED, HALVED

150G (4½ OUNCES) SNOW PEAS

1 TABLESPOON FINELY GRATED FRESH GINGER

¼ CUP (60ML) SOY SAUCE

2 TABLESPOONS MIRIN

1 TEASPOON SESAME OIL

1 GREEN ONION (SCALLION), EXTRA, SLICED THINLY

2 TEASPOONS BLACK SESAME SEEDS

1 Preheat oven to 200°C/400°F.

2 Cook noodles in a large saucepan of boiling salted water for 3 minutes or until just tender. Drain; keep warm.

3 Combine miso, vinegar, syrup and half the vegetable oil in a large bowl. Add salmon; toss to coat. Arrange green onion, side-by-side, on an oven tray; place salmon on top. Drizzle with remaining vegetable oil. Roast for 10 minutes or until salmon is cooked as desired.

4 Meanwhile, boil, steam or microwave snow peas until just tender; drain. Refresh in a bowl of iced water; drain.

5 Place noodles in a medium bowl with ginger, soy sauce, mirin and sesame oil; toss to coat. Flake salmon onto noodles, add cooked green onion and snow peas; toss gently to combine. Serve topped with extra green onion and sesame seeds.

prep + cook time 30 minutes (+ cooling) **serves** 4
nutritional count per serving 18.2g total fat (3.1g saturated fat); 2443kJ (583 cal); 64g carbohydrate; 39g protein; 3.4g fibre
tip Salmon can be refrigerated in the marinade up to 3 hours before cooking.

LAMB KOFTA
With WHITE BEANS

400G (12½ OUNCES) CANNED WHITE BEANS, DRAINED, RINSED

1 TABLESPOON LEMON JUICE

2 TABLESPOONS FRESH OREGANO LEAVES

2 TABLESPOONS OLIVE OIL

½ CUP (35G) FRESH BREADCRUMBS

2 TABLESPOON MILK

600G (1¼ POUNDS) MINCED (GROUND) LAMB

1 TEASPOON GROUND ALLSPICE

⅓ CUP FRESH OREGANO LEAVES, EXTRA, CHOPPED COARSELY

100G (3 OUNCES) FETTA, CRUMBLED

1 BABY COS (ROMAINE) LETTUCE, TRIMMED, LEAVES SEPARATED

BEETROOT TZATZIKI

200G (6½ OUNCES) BEETROOT (BEETS), PEELED, GRATED COARSELY

1 CUP (280G) GREEK-STYLE YOGHURT

2 TABLESPOONS CHOPPED FRESH MINT

1 CLOVE GARLIC, CRUSHED

1 TABLESPOON FINELY GRATED LEMON RIND

1 Make beetroot tzatiki.

2 Combine white beans, juice, oregano and half the oil in a medium bowl. Season to taste.

3 Place breadcrumbs and milk in a medium bowl; stand for 3 minutes or until milk has been absorbed. Add lamb, allspice and extra oregano; season. Using your hands, work mixture until well combined. Add fetta; stir until combined. Roll heaped tablespoonful measures of lamb mixture into kofta shapes.

4 Heat remaining oil in a large non-stick frying pan over medium-high heat; cook kofta, turning occasionally, for 10 minutes or until browned and cooked through.

5 Serve kofta on lettuce with bean mixture and tzatziki.

beetroot tzatziki Combine ingredients in a medium bowl; season to taste.

prep + cook time 40 minutes (+ cooling) **serves** 4
nutritional count per serving 41g total fat (16.4g saturated fat); 2680kJ (640 cal); 21.4g carbohydrate; 44.5g protein; 4.9g fibre
tip Cooked or uncooked kofta can be frozen for up to 3 months. Thaw in the fridge.

I AM
LOW FAT
PROTEIN RICH
LOW GI

PEA & BARLEY RISOTTO
With GARLIC PRAWNS

1 TABLESPOON OLIVE OIL

1 FRESH LONG RED CHILLI, CHOPPED FINELY

2 CLOVES GARLIC, CHOPPED

2 SHALLOTS (50G), CHOPPED FINELY

1 CUP (200G) PEARL BARLEY

1 LITRE (4 CUPS) CHICKEN STOCK

1 CUP (250ML) WATER

1 TABLESPOON FINELY GRATED LEMON RIND

½ CUP (60G) FROZEN PEAS

150G (4½ OUNCES) SUGAR SNAP PEAS, TRIMMED, HALVED LENGTHWAYS

2 TABLESPOONS OLIVE OIL, EXTRA

400G (12½ OUNCES) PEELED UNCOOKED PRAWNS (SHRIMP), TAILS INTACT, BUTTERFLIED

2 CLOVES GARLIC, EXTRA, CRUSHED

SNOW PEA TENDRILS AND THIN STRIPS LEMON RIND, TO SERVE (OPTIONAL)

1 Heat oil in a large saucepan over medium-low heat, add chilli, garlic and shallots; cook, stirring, for 3 minutes or until tender. Add barley; cook, stirring for 2 minutes or until lightly toasted. Add half the stock; bring to the boil. Reduce heat to low; cook, stirring occasionally, for 18 minutes or until the liquid has been absorbed. Add remaining stock and the water; cook, stirring occasionally for a further 18 minutes or until most of the liquid has been absorbed. Add rind, peas and sugar snap peas; cook, stirring, for 3 minutes or until vegetables are tender. Season.

2 Meanwhile, heat extra oil in a medium frying pan over high heat; cook prawns and extra garlic, stirring, for 5 minutes or until prawns are just cooked. Season.

3 Serve risotto topped with prawns, snow pea tendrils and lemon rind strips.

prep + cook time 1 hour **serves** 4

nutritional count per serving 16.7g total fat (2.8g saturated fat); 1766kJ (422 cal); 35g carbohydrate; 28.1g protein; 9.6g fibre

tip Risotto is best made just before serving.

The greatest quantities of potent omega-3 fatty acids are to be found in oily fish, such as TUNA, HERRING, MACKEREL, SARDINES and SALMON.

Evidence suggests omega-3 fatty acids can make us smarter and keep us smart. Brain development in infants whose mothers ate oily fish during pregnancy is improved, and as we age it may reduce our chances of cognitive impairment and dementia.

Oysters

OYSTERS CONTAIN THE RICHEST FOOD SOURCE OF ZINC. IN FACT A SINGLE OYSTER (OR TWO IN THE CASE OF MEN) MEETS THE RECOMMENDED DAILY INTAKE FOR THIS NUTRIENT.

SMART CHOICES

When is comes to eating fish, we need to make smart choices. For sustainability, choose smaller fish, lower down the food chain, as stocks of smaller species are generally more quickly replenished than those of large game fish (shark, blue fin tuna, swordfish, marlin) that take years to reach their size. In addition, the longer life span of large fish leads to a greater accumulation of mercury and other heavy metals that may be damaging to our health.

PRAWNS LIKE ALL SEAFOOD PROVIDE GOOD LEVELS OF LONG CHAIN OMEGA-3 FATS. CHOOSE PRAWNS FROM LOCAL FISHERIES FOR THEIR SUSTAINABLE PRACTICES AND AVOID IMPORTED PRAWNS AS THESE HAVE BEEN ASSIGNED RED RATING DUE TO CONCERNS IN FISH HUSBANDRY.

BY INCLUDING *two servings* OF FISH (PARTICULARLY OILY TYPES) IN OUR DIET, PER WEEK WE CAN *reduce our risk* OF CARDIOVASCULAR DISEASE.

SEAFOOD

I AM

HIGH IN IRON

PROTEIN RICH

LOW FAT

FISH CONTAIN *unsaturated fatty acids* THAT ARE THOUGHT TO *lower cholesterol* LEVELS AND REDUCE INFLAMMATION. SHELLFISH, SUCH AS MUSSELS, CLAMS AND OYSTERS ARE COLLECTIVELY *rich in minerals* IN PARTICULAR ZINC, IRON AND SELENIUM.

KOREAN BEEF *And* CORN
SOFT TACOS

6 WOMBOK (NAPA CABBAGE) LEAVES (450G), TRIMMED, CUT INTO LARGE PIECES

2 TABLESPOONS SEA SALT FLAKES

2 TABLESPOONS RICE VINEGAR

2 TEASPOONS KOREAN CHILLI PASTE (GOCHUJANG)

2 TABLESPOONS RICE MALT SYRUP

1 TEASPOON SESAME OIL

½ MEDIUM BROWN ONION (75G), GRATED COARSELY

2 CLOVES GARLIC, GRATED FINELY

¼ CUP (60ML) SOY SAUCE

¼ CUP (60ML) RICE MALT SYRUP, EXTRA

1 TABLESPOON SESAME OIL, EXTRA

750G (1½ POUNDS) BEEF FLANK (SKIRT) STEAK, BUTTERFLIED TO 1.5CM (¾-INCH) THICK

2 CORN COBS (800G), TRIMMED, HUSK AND SILKS REMOVED

8 X 15CM (6-INCH) CORN TORTILLAS (200G), WARMED

1 LARGE AVOCADO (320G), SLICED THINLY

MICRO HERBS, TO SERVE (OPTIONAL)

1 To make the spicy kimchi, wash wombok then toss with salt in a colander. Place colander over a bowl; stand for 30 minutes. Rinse wombok well to remove the salt; pat dry with paper towel. Combine rice vinegar, paste, syrup and oil in a large bowl. Add wombok; toss well to coat. Set aside.

2 Meanwhile, combine onion, garlic, soy sauce, extra syrup and extra oil in a medium bowl; season. Add steak; mix well to coat. Cover; refrigerate for 1 hour.

3 Cook corn on an oiled grill plate (or grill or barbecue) over high heat for 10 minutes, turning occasionally, or until lightly charred. Remove from heat. When cool enough to handle, cut kernels from cobs.

4 Drain steak; discard marinade. Cook steak on an oiled grill plate (or grill or barbecue) over medium-high heat for 3 minutes each side for medium rare or until cooked to your liking. Remove from heat; rest, covered, for 5 minutes. Slice thinly.

5 Divide spicy kimchi, corn, avocado and steak among tortillas; top with micro herbs.

prep + cook time 40 minutes (+ standing & refrigeration)
serves 4
nutritional count per serving 37.9g total fat (10.6g saturated fat); 3717kJ (888 cal); 63.1g carbohydrate; 63.8g protein; 14.7g fibre
tip If you can't get flank or skirt steak, rump steak can also be used.

I AM

DAIRY FREE

PROTEIN RICH

LOW CARB

LAMB BACKSTRAP
with WARM MUSHROOM SALAD

15G (½ OUNCE) DRIED PORCINI MUSHROOMS

1 CUP (250ML) WARM WATER

2 TABLESPOONS OLIVE OIL

1 MEDIUM BROWN ONION (150G), CHOPPED FINELY

2 CLOVES GARLIC, CRUSHED

4 SLICES PANCETTA (60G), CHOPPED

200G (6½ OUNCES) SWISS BROWN MUSHROOMS, HALVED HORIZONTALLY

400G (12½ OUNCES) CANNED LENTILS, DRAINED, RINSED

400G (12½ OUNCES) MIXED BABY TOMATOES

⅓ CUP COARSELY CHOPPED FRESH FLAT-LEAF PARSLEY

4 LAMB BACKSTRAPS (EYE OF LOIN) (800G)

1 TABLESPOON FRESH THYME LEAVES

125G (4 OUNCES) ROCKET (ARUGULA)

1 Place porcini mushrooms and the warm water in a small bowl; stand for 20 minutes or until tender. Drain; reserve ⅓ cup (80ml) of the soaking liquid.

2 Heat half the oil in a large saucepan over medium-high heat; cook onion, garlic and pancetta, stirring, for 5 minutes or until softened.

3 Add swiss brown mushrooms to pan; cook, stirring occasionally, for 5 minutes or until almost tender. Add lentils, tomatoes, porcini mushrooms and reserved soaking liquid; cook, stirring for 5 minutes or until tomatoes start to soften. Stir in parsley.

4 Meanwhile, rub lamb with remaining oil; sprinkle with thyme. Cook lamb on a heated oiled grill plate (or grill or barbecue) for 5 minutes, turning halfway through cooking time, or until cooked as desired. Remove from heat; rest, covered, for 5 minutes. Slice thickly.

5 Serve lamb on warm salad with rocket.

prep + cook time 40 minutes (+ standing) **serves** 4
nutritional count per serving 23.9g total fat (6.3g saturated fat); 2108kJ (503 cal); 11.4g carbohydrate; 57g protein; 7.1g fibre
tip Use lamb tenderloin if backstrap is unavailable.

PRAWN BITES
with MANGO SALAD

300G (9½ OUNCES) PEELED UNCOOKED PRAWNS (SHRIMP)

200G (6½ OUNCES) BONELESS FIRM WHITE FISH FILLETS, CHOPPED COARSELY

1 FREE-RANGE EGG WHITE

2 TEASPOONS FISH SAUCE

⅓ CUP (50G) CORNFLOUR (CORNSTARCH)

¼ CUP FINELY CHOPPED FRESH CORIANDER (CILANTRO) ROOT AND STEMS

1 TABLESPOON RICE BRAN OIL

1 BUTTER (BOSTON) LETTUCE, LEAVES SEPARATED

CORIANDER SAUCE

1 CUP LOOSELY PACKED FRESH CORIANDER (CILANTRO) LEAVES

½ CUP LOOSELY PACKED FRESH FLAT-LEAF PARSLEY LEAVES

2 TABLESPOONS ROASTED CASHEWS

2 TABLESPOONS LIME JUICE

¼ CUP (60ML) OLIVE OIL

1 CLOVE GARLIC, CRUSHED

1 TABLESPOON WATER

MANGO SALAD

1 MEDIUM MANGO (430G), SLICED THINLY

1 MEDIUM CARROT (120G), SLICED THINLY

1 CUP (80G) BEAN SPROUTS

½ CUP LOOSELY PACKED FRESH CORIANDER (CILANTRO) LEAVES

2 TABLESPOONS UNSALTED ROASTED CASHEWS, CHOPPED COARSELY

1 FRESH LONG RED CHILLI, SEEDED, SLICED THINLY

1 Make coriander sauce, then mango salad.

2 Process prawns, fish, egg white, fish sauce, cornflour and coriander root and stem mixture in a food processor until chopped coarsely and combined.

3 Heat oil in a large non-stick frying pan over medium-high heat; cook level tablespoons of prawn mixture for 8 minutes or until browned and cooked through.

4 Serve mango salad and prawn bites on lettuce leaves with remaining coriander sauce.

coriander sauce Blend or process ingredients until smooth; season to taste.

mango salad Place ingredients in a medium bowl with 2 tablespoons of coriander sauce; toss to combine. Season to taste.

prep + cook time 50 minutes **serves** 4

nutritional count per serving 26g total fat (4.2g saturated fat); 1967kJ (470 cal); 25g carbohydrate; 30.8g protein; 6.1g fibre

tip Coriander sauce and mango salad are also great served with grilled chicken.

I AM

VITAMIN RICH

PROTEIN RICH

DAIRY FREE

I AM

GLUTEN FREE

PROTEIN RICH

DAIRY FREE

TO BRUISE GARLIC, PRESS THE SIDE OF A LARGE COOK'S KNIFE ON EACH CLOVE UNTIL IT SPLITS. WHEN FRESH FIGS ARE OUT OF SEASON, SOAK HALVED DRIED FIGS IN BOILING WATER FOR 15 MINUTES AND USE INSTEAD.

STICKY CHICKEN DRUMSTICKS
With FENNEL And FRESH FIGS

1KG (2 POUNDS) CHICKEN DRUMSTICKS

3 BABY FENNEL BULBS (390G), SLICED THICKLY, FRONDS RESERVED

8 CLOVES GARLIC, UNPEELED, BRUISED

2 TABLESPOONS FRESH ROSEMARY LEAVES

1 TEASPOON FINELY GRATED LEMON RIND

¼ CUP (90G) HONEY

¼ CUP (60ML) EXTRA VIRGIN OLIVE OIL

2 TABLESPOONS HONEY, EXTRA

30G (1 OUNCE) BABY ROCKET (ARUGULA) LEAVES

6 MEDIUM FRESH FIGS (360G), TORN IN HALF

2 TABLESPOONS LEMON JUICE

1 Combine chicken, sliced fennel, garlic, rosemary, rind, honey and half the oil in a large dish. Cover; refrigerate for 2 hours.

2 Preheat oven to 220°C/425°F. Line a large oven tray with baking paper.

3 Transfer chicken, sliced fennel, garlic and rosemary to tray, in a single layer; discard marinade. Drizzle chicken with extra honey; season. Roast, brushing occasionally with pan juices, for 40 minutes or until chicken is cooked through.

4 Meanwhile, combine 1 tablespoon of the remaining oil with rocket, figs and juice in a medium bowl; season.

5 Serve chicken mixture with rocket salad and reserved fennel fronds; drizzle with remaining oil.

prep + cook time 55 minutes (+ refrigeration) **serves** 4
nutritional count per serving 29.1g total fat (6.8g saturated fat); 2298kJ (549 cal); 40.5g carbohydrate; 30.6g protein; 5.3g fibre

WE USED THE SMALL LEAVES FROM THE BUNCH OF BEETROOT, BUT YOU CAN USE MIXED BABY SALAD LEAVES INSTEAD.

BARBECUED KANGAROO STEAKS
with BEETROOT SALAD

1KG (2 POUNDS) BABY BEETROOT (BEETS)

8 SHALLOTS (200G), UNPEELED

¼ CUP (60ML) EXTRA VIRGIN OLIVE OIL

4 X 180G (5½-OUNCE) KANGAROO STEAKS

1 TABLESPOONS FINELY CHOPPED ROSEMARY

200G (6½ OUNCES) BABY BEETROOT (BEETS) LEAVES

¼ CUP (25G) ROASTED WALNUTS, CHOPPED

ROSEMARY YOGHURT DRESSING

½ CUP (140G) GREEK-STYLE YOGHURT

1 TEASPOON FINELY CHOPPED FRESH ROSEMARY LEAVES

1 TABLESPOON HONEY

1 TABLESPOON DIJON MUSTARD

1 TABLESPOON EXTRA VIRGIN OLIVE OIL

1 Make rosemary yoghurt dressing.

2 Place beetroot and shallots in the centre of two large pieces of foil, drizzle with 1 tablespoon of the oil; season. Fold foil into parcels to completely enclose vegetables. Place parcels on one side of a heated oiled grill plate (or grill or barbecue) over medium heat for 35 minutes, turning every 10 minutes, or until beetroot and shallots are tender.

3 Meanwhile, coat steaks in remaining oil; sprinkle with rosemary. Season. Cook steaks on the other side of the grill plate; cook for 2 minutes each side or until cooked as desired. Remove from heat; rest, covered, for 5 minutes.

4 Peel beetroot and shallots, then cut in half; place in a medium bowl with leaves and nuts, then toss to combine.

5 Serve sliced steak with salad, drizzled with dressing.

rosemary yoghurt dressing Place ingredients in a screw-top jar; shake well. Season. Refrigerate until needed.

prep + cook time 50 minutes **serves** 4
nutritional count per serving 27.9g total fat (5.2g saturated fat); 2439kJ (582 cal); 32g carbohydrate; 47.5g protein; 9g fibre

I AM

LOW CARB

PROTEIN RICH

PALEO

STORING BABY CARROTS WITH THE LEAVES ATTACHED REDUCES THEIR KEEPING TIME DRAMATICALLY. CUT THE TOPS OFF AS SOON AS YOU CAN. WRAP THE TOPS IN DAMP PAPER TOWEL; REFRIGERATE UNTIL NEEDED.

IRISH STEW
with CARROT-TOP SALSA VERDE

⅓ CUP (80ML) OLIVE OIL

1KG (2 POUNDS) BONED LAMB NECK, CUT INTO 5CM (2-INCH) PIECES

1 MEDIUM BROWN ONION (150G), CHOPPED

1 TRIMMED CELERY STALK (100G), CHOPPED FINELY

3 CLOVES GARLIC, CRUSHED

1.25 LITRES (5 CUPS) CHICKEN STOCK

400G (12½ OUNCES) BABY (DUTCH) CARROTS WITH TOPS, TRIMMED, TOPS RESERVED

1 MEDIUM SWEDE (225G), CUT INTO SIX WEDGES

½ CUP (70G) ROASTED HAZELNUTS, CHOPPED

CARROT-TOP SALSA VERDE

1½ CUPS LOOSELY PACKED FRESH FLAT-LEAF PARSLEY LEAVES

1½ TABLESPOONS LOOSELY PACKED FRESH LEMON THYME LEAVES

1 TABLESPOON DRAINED CAPERS

1 SMALL CLOVE GARLIC, CRUSHED

1 TEASPOON LIGHT BROWN SUGAR

½ CUP (125ML) EXTRA VIRGIN OLIVE OIL

1½ TABLESPOONS WHITE WINE VINEGAR

1 Heat 2 tablespoons of the oil in a large heavy-based saucepan over high heat; cook lamb, in batches, for 5 minutes, turning occasionally, until browned all over. Remove from pan. (If the base of the pan starts to burn, add 2 tablespoons water and stir to lift the meat sticking on the base of the pan.)

2 Reduce heat to medium, add remaining oil to pan; cook onion, celery and garlic, stirring occasionally, for 10 minutes or until softened. Return lamb to pan with stock; bring to the boil. Reduce heat to low; simmer, covered, for 2 hours or until meat is tender.

3 Meanwhile, wash reserved carrot tops; you need ½ cup firmly packed tops for salsa verde, and extra to serve.

4 Make carrot-top salsa verde.

5 Increase pan heat to high; return to the boil. Add carrots and swede; simmer, uncovered, for 15 minutes or until liquid has thickened slightly. Season. Serve topped with hazelnuts, salsa verde and extra carrot tops.

carrot-top salsa verde Blend or process ingredients with the reserved ½ cup carrot tops (from step 3), until well combined; season. Refrigerate until needed.

prep + cook time 2 hours 20 minutes serves 4
nutritional count per serving 73.3g total fat (15g saturated fat); 4011kJ (958 cal); 12.8g carbohydrate; 57.7g protein; 11.9g fibre

RED WINE BRAISED SALMON
with ROOT VEGETABLE WEDGES

3 CUPS (750ML) RED WINE

2 TABLESPOONS HONEY

2 CLOVES GARLIC, CRUSHED

4 LONG STRIPS ORANGE RIND

1KG (2 POUNDS) SIDE OF SALMON,
SKIN ON, BONED

3 SMALL PARSNIPS (360G), QUARTERED
LENGTHWAYS

1 SMALL PURPLE SWEET POTATO (250G),
CUT INTO SIXTHS LENGTHWAYS

1 SMALL KUMARA (ORANGE SWEET POTATO) (250G),
CUT INTO SIXTHS LENGTHWAYS

2 TABLESPOONS OLIVE OIL

¼ CUP (25G) ROASTED WALNUTS, CHOPPED

MICRO PARSLEY AND RADISH LEAVES, TO SERVE

RED WINE VINEGAR & HONEY DRESSING

2 TABLESPOONS RED WINE VINEGAR

¼ CUP (60ML) FRESHLY SQUEEZED
ORANGE JUICE

2 TABLESPOONS HONEY

1 SMALL CLOVE GARLIC, CRUSHED

1 Combine wine, honey, garlic and rind in a medium deep-sided baking dish; add salmon, skin-side up. Cover; refrigerate for 2 hours, turning halfway through.

2 Preheat oven to 200°C/400°F. Grease two large oven trays; line with baking paper.

3 Combine parsnip, sweet potato, kumara and oil in a medium bowl; season. Spread evenly between trays. Roast, turning occasionally, for 40 minutes or until tender. Cover to keep warm.

4 Meanwhile, make red wine vinegar and honey dressing.

5 Bake salmon, skin-side up, for 12 minutes or until just cooked through. Drain salmon; discard liquid. Invert salmon onto a serving platter.

6 Top salmon with dressing, walnuts and micro herbs. Serve immediately with vegetable wedges.

red wine vinegar & honey dressing Place ingredients in a small saucepan over high heat; bring to the boil. Cook, stirring occasionally, for 5 minutes or until thickened slightly, strain; season to taste.

prep + cook time 1 hour (+ refrigeration) **serves** 6
nutritional count per serving 27.3g total fat (6.4g saturated fat); 2794kJ (667 cal); 38.7g carbohydrate; 51g protein; 4.5g fibre

tips Before serving, return the wedges to the oven for 5 minutes to reheat while you drain the salmon. A shiraz or cabernet sauvignon would be great to use in this recipe, but any red wine will be fine.

I AM

ANTIOXIDANTS

HIGH IN OMEGA 3

PROTEIN RICH

BONE BROTH

FISH BROTH

prep + cook time 25 minutes (+ cooling & refrigeration)
makes 2 litres (8 cups)

Place 1.5kg (3lbs) fish bones, 3 litres (12 cups) water, 1 coarsely chopped onion, 2 coarsely chopped trimmed celery stalks, 6 stalks fresh flat-leaf parsley and 1 teaspoon black peppercorns in a large saucepan; bring to the boil. Reduce heat; simmer, uncovered, for 30 minutes. Strain stock through a muslin-lined sieve into heatproof bowl; discard solids. Season with sea salt and 2 tablespoons lemon juice. Cool. Cover; refrigerate until cold. Skim and discard any surface fat before use.

CHICKEN BROTH

prep + cook time 6¼ hours (+ cooling & refrigeration)
makes 3 litres (12 cups)

Place 2kg (4lbs) chicken bones, 2 tablespoons cider vinegar, 2 coarsely chopped medium onions, 2 coarsely chopped trimmed celery stalks, 2 coarsely chopped medium carrots, 8 peeled cloves garlic, 6 stalks fresh flat-leaf parsley, 2 teaspoons black peppercorns and 5 litres (20 cups) water in a large saucepan; bring to the boil. Reduce heat; simmer, uncovered, for 6 hours, skimming the surface occasionally. Strain stock through a muslin-lined sieve into a heatproof bowl; discard solids. Season with sea salt. Cool. Cover; refrigerate until cold. Skim and discard surface fat before using.

BEEF BROTH

prep + cook time 8¼ hours (+ cooling & refrigeration)

makes 2 litres (8 cups)

Preheat oven to 200°C/400°F. Roast 2kg (4lbs) beef bones on a large oven tray, uncovered, for 1 hour or until browned. Place bones in a large saucepan with 2 chopped unpeeled brown onions, 2 coarsely chopped trimmed celery stalks, 2 chopped carrots, 8 cloves peeled garlic, 2 tablespoons cider vinegar, 2 teaspoons black peppercorns and 5 litres (20 cups) water; bring to the boil. Reduce heat; simmer, uncovered, for 8 hours, skimming the surface occasionally. Strain stock through a muslin-lined sieve into a heatproof bowl; discard solids. Add extra water to make up 2 litres. Season with sea salt. Cool. Cover; refrigerate until cold. Skim and discard surface fat before using.

VEGETABLE BROTH

prep + cook time 1¾ hours (+ cooling & refrigeration)

makes 3 litres (12 cups)

Place 4 coarsely chopped onions, 2 coarsely chopped large carrots, 8 coarsely chopped trimmed celery stalks, 2 coarsely chopped large parsnips, 8 peeled cloves garlic, 6 stalks fresh flat-leaf parsley, 2 teaspoons black peppercorns and 4 litres (16 cups) water in a large saucepan; bring to the boil. Reduce heat; simmer, uncovered, for 1½ hours. Add 200g (6½oz) coarsely chopped cup mushrooms and 4 coarsely chopped tomatoes; simmer, uncovered, for a further 30 minutes. Strain stock through a muslin-lined sieve into a heatproof bowl; discard solids. Season with sea salt. Cool. Cover; refrigerate until cold.

I AM
**GREAT FOR
GUT HEALTH**

HAVE YOUR BROTH VERY HOT FOR SERVING, AS THE HEAT OF THE SOUP WILL COOK THE SALMON IN THE SERVING BOWL.

SALMON PHO
with KELP NOODLES

3 LITRES (12 CUPS) FISH STOCK

2 STAR ANISE

2 TEASPOONS FINELY GRATED FRESH GINGER

1 CINNAMON STICK

2 CORIANDER ROOTS, BRUISED

454G (14½ OUNCES) KELP NOODLES

1½ CUPS (120G) BEAN SPROUTS

¼ CUP FRESH CORIANDER (CILANTRO) LEAVES

¼ CUP FRESH MINT LEAVES

¼ CUP FRESH THAI BASIL LEAVES

2 GREEN ONIONS (SCALLIONS), SLICED THINLY ON THE DIAGONAL

2 FRESH LONG RED CHILLIES, SLICED THINLY ON THE DIAGONAL

¼ CUP (60ML) FISH SAUCE

750G (1½ POUNDS) SASHIMI GRADE SALMON, SKINLESS, BONED, CUT INTO 5MM (¼-INCH) SLICES

1 MEDIUM LEMON (140G), CUT INTO 6 WEDGES

1 Place stock, star anise, ginger, cinnamon and coriander roots in a large saucepan; bring to the boil. Reduce heat to low; simmer for 10 minutes.

2 Meanwhile, cook noodles in another large saucepan of boiling water for 10 minutes or until softened slightly; drain well.

3 Combine sprouts, herbs, green onion and chilli in a medium bowl.

4 Strain broth though a fine sieve into another large saucepan. Bring to the boil over high heat; stir in fish sauce.

5 Divide noodles and salmon among soup bowls; ladle hot broth into bowls and top with sprout mixture. Serve with lemon wedges.

prep + cook time 30 minutes **serves** 4

nutritional count per serving 26.8g total fat (6.9g saturated fat); 2205kJ (526 cal); 10g carbohydrate; 60.9g protein; 2.5g fibre

tips Kelp noodles are high in iodine and are gluten-free and low carb; they can be found in health food stores and some Asian supermarkets. You can use mung bean thread noodles or glass rice vermicelli noodles instead, if you like.

I AM
LOW CARB
HIGH IN IRON
PALEO

YOU CAN USE 2KG (4 POUNDS) MUSSELS IF YOU CAN'T FIND PIPIS, AND USE REGULAR BASIL INSTEAD OF THAI BASIL, IF YOU PREFER.

PIPIS & MUSSELS
WITH GINGER AND LIME

1KG (2 POUNDS) PIPIS

1 CUP (250ML) SALT-REDUCED VEGETABLE OR CHICKEN STOCK

3 FRESH KAFFIR LIME LEAVES, TORN

1KG (2 POUNDS) SMALL BLACK MUSSELS, SCRUBBED, BEARDS REMOVED

2 TABLESPOONS VEGETABLE OIL

2 CLOVES GARLIC, CRUSHED

1 FRESH LONG RED CHILLI, CHOPPED FINELY

20G (¾-OUNCE) PIECE FRESH GINGER, CUT INTO THIN MATCHSTICKS

4 FRESH KAFFIR LIME LEAVES, EXTRA, SHREDDED

1 TABLESPOON FISH SAUCE

1 TABLESPOON OYSTER SAUCE

1 CUP FRESH CORIANDER (CILANTRO) LEAVES

1 CUP FRESH THAI BASIL LEAVES

1 Soak pipis in a large bowl of cold water for 3 minutes; drain well.

2 Heat a wok over high heat, add pipis, stock and lime leaves; cook, covered, stirring occasionally, for 5 minutes or until pipis begin to open. Remove pipis with tongs as they open, discard pipis that remain closed. Repeat process with mussels.

3 Strain stock through a fine sieve into a small heatproof bowl; discard solids. Reserve stock.

4 Heat oil in wok over high heat; cook garlic, chilli, ginger and extra lime leaves, stirring occasionally, for 1 minute or until fragrant. Add sauces and 1 cup (250ml) of the reserved stock; cook, stirring, for 2 minutes or until thickened slightly. Add pipis and mussels; cook, stirring for 1 minute or until heated through. Stir in herbs, serve immediately.

prep + cook time 20 minutes **serves** 4

nutritional count per serving 11.5g total fat (1.7g saturated fat); 805kJ (192 cal); 7.9g carbohydrate; 13.4g protein; 1.6g fibre

serving suggestion Serve with cooked thai red rice or black rice, both can be found at Asian supermarkets.

ROASTED SUMAC CHICKEN

with BABY VEGETABLES

30G (1 OUNCE) BUTTER, SOFTENED

1 TABLESPOON GROUND SUMAC

1.4KG (2¾-POUND) WHOLE CHICKEN

500G (1 POUND) BABY BEETROOT (BEETS), TRIMMED

250G (8 OUNCES) BABY (DUTCH) CARROTS, TRIMMED

250G (8 OUNCES) BABY PURPLE CARROTS, TRIMMED

1 TABLESPOON OLIVE OIL

1 MEDIUM BLOOD ORANGE (240G), PEELED, SLICED THICKLY

½ CUP FRESH MINT LEAVES

100G (3 OUNCES) FETTA, CRUMBLED

2 TABLESPOONS PISTACHIO DUKKAH

1 Preheat oven to 180°C/350°F.

2 Combine butter and sumac in a small bowl. Massage sumac butter all over the outside of the chicken. Tie chicken legs together with kitchen string; season. Place in a large baking dish. Wrap beetroot individually in foil; add to dish with chicken. Roast for 30 minutes.

3 Baste chicken with pan juices. Toss carrots in oil; season and add to dish. Roast for a further 30 minutes, or until chicken is cooked through and skin is golden brown. Loosely cover chicken with foil; rest 10 minutes.

4 Meanwhile, peel beetroot and cut in half. Return beetroot to pan with blood orange and mint.

5 Serve chicken and vegetables with fetta and dukkah.

prep + cook time 1 hour 15 minutes **serves** 4
nutritional count per serving 40.3g total fat (13.9g saturated fat); 2740kJ (654 cal); 22.2g carbohydrate; 47g protein; 9.3g fibre
tip Use goat's fetta or ricotta, if you prefer.

I AM
HIGH IN IRON
PROTEIN RICH
LOW CARB

NUT-CRUSTED BARRAMUNDI
WITH SPICED KUMARA WEDGES

¾ CUP (120G) BRAZIL NUTS

¼ CUP (20G) NATURAL FLAKED ALMONDS

2 TEASPOONS FINELY GRATED FRESH GINGER

2 TEASPOONS FINELY GRATED LIME RIND

4 X 180G (5½-OUNCE) SKINLESS
BARRAMUNDI FILLETS

100G (3 OUNCES) SUGAR SNAP PEAS,
TRIMMED

MICRO HERBS, TO SERVE (OPTIONAL)

SPICED KUMARA WEDGES

3 SMALL KUMARA (ORANGE SWEET POTATO)
(500G), CUT INTO THIN WEDGES

2 TEASPOONS RED CURRY PASTE

2 TEASPOONS LIGHT BROWN SUGAR

2 TABLESPOON COARSELY CHOPPED
FRESH CORIANDER (CILANTRO)

COCONUT DRESSING

½ CUP (125ML) COCONUT CREAM

2 TABLESPOONS LIME JUICE

1 TABLESPOON FISH SAUCE

2 TEASPOONS LIGHT BROWN SUGAR
(OR COCONUT SUGAR)

1 FRESH LONG RED CHILLI, SEEDED,
CHOPPED FINELY

1 Preheat oven to 200°C/400°F. Line an oven tray with baking paper.

2 Place brazil nuts, almonds, ginger and rind in a food processor; pulse until mixture forms a chunky paste.

3 Make spiced kumara wedges.

4 Place fillets on oven tray; season. Press nut mixture evenly on each fillet. Bake fish alongside kumara for 10 minutes or until crust is golden brown.

5 Meanwhile, place sugar snap peas in a colander in the sink; pour boiling water over peas. Drain well; refresh under cold running water.

6 Make coconut dressing.

7 Serve fillets topped with micro herbs and dressing, sugar snap peas and kumara wedges.

spiced kumara wedges Combine kumara, curry paste and sugar; spread on a baking-paper-lined oven tray. Bake for 30 minutes, turning halfway, until tender. Sprinkle with coriander.

coconut dressing Combine ingredients in a small jug.

prep + cook time 40 minutes **serves** 4

nutritional count per serving 31.9g total fat (10.7g saturated fat); 2596kJ (620 cal); 31.2g carbohydrate; 48.6g protein; 7.8g fibre

tip Recipe is best made just before serving.

THE CREAMY CAULIFLOWER SAUCE CAN ALSO BE SERVED WITH GRILLED SEAFOOD OR CHICKEN. OR REDUCE THE MILK TO ¼ CUP FOR A THICKER CAULIFLOWER MASH RATHER THAN A PURÉE.

SPELT PASTA
With SILKY CAULIFLOWER SAUCE

1KG (2 POUNDS) CAULIFLOWER, CUT INTO FLORETS

1 CUP (250ML) VEGETABLE STOCK

2 CLOVES GARLIC, PEELED

2 TABLESPOONS EXTRA VIRGIN OLIVE OIL

¾ CUP (45G) MULTIGRAIN BREADCRUMBS

1 FRESH LONG RED CHILLI, SEEDED, CHOPPED FINELY

1 CLOVE GARLIC, EXTRA, CRUSHED

¼ CUP CHOPPED FRESH FLAT-LEAF PARSLEY

1 TABLESPOON FINELY GRATED LEMON RIND

375G (12 OUNCES) DRIED SPELT FETTUCCINE PASTA

½ CUP (40G) GRATED PARMESAN

2 TABLESPOONS EXTRA VIRGIN OLIVE OIL, EXTRA

1½ CUPS (375ML) MILK

¾ CUP (60G) GRATED PARMESAN, EXTRA

1 TABLESPOON LEMON JUICE

1 Place three-quarters of the cauliflower in a medium saucepan with stock and garlic; bring to the boil. Reduce heat; simmer, covered, for 10 minutes or until cauliflower is tender.

2 Meanwhile, cut remaining cauliflower into tiny florets. Heat oil in a large frying pan over high heat, add florets; cook stirring, for 2 minutes until lightly golden. Add breadcrumbs, chilli and extra garlic; cook, stirring for 2 minutes, or until breadcrumbs are golden and crisp. Remove from heat; stir in parsley and rind.

3 Cook pasta in a large saucepan of boiling salted water following packet instructions. Drain well; return to pan with parmesan and extra oil.

4 Blend cauliflower stock mixture with milk until very smooth. Stir in extra parmesan and juice. Season to taste.

5 Spoon cauliflower sauce over pasta; serve topped with toasted cauliflower crumbs.

prep + cook time 40 minutes **serves** 4

nutritional count per serving 32.8g total fat (10.7g saturated fat); 3312kJ (791 cal); 73.3g carbohydrate; 32.6g protein; 7.5g fibre

I AM
VEGETARIAN
PROTEIN RICH
HIGH FIBRE

RED LENTIL DHAL
With CASHEW TOPPING

1 TABLESPOON GHEE

1 LARGE RED ONION (300G), CHOPPED

4 CLOVES GARLIC, CHOPPED FINELY

20G (¾-OUNCE) PIECE FRESH GINGER, CHOPPED FINELY

10G (½-OUNCE) PIECE FRESH TURMERIC, GRATED OR ½ TEASPOON GROUND TURMERIC

2 TEASPOONS GARAM MASALA

1 CUP (200G) DRY RED LENTILS

2 MEDIUM TOMATOES (300G), CHOPPED

2 FRESH LONG GREEN CHILIES, SLICED THINLY

1 LITRE (4 CUPS) WATER

750G (1½ POUNDS) CAULIFLOWER, CUT INTO FLORETS

1 MEDIUM PARSNIP (250G), CHOPPED FINELY

600G (1¼ OUNCES) RAINBOW CHARD, CUT INTO 3CM (1¼-INCH) PIECES

½ CUP (140G) GREEK-STYLE YOGHURT

4 PAPPADUMS (8G)

CASHEW TOPPING

1 TABLESPOON GHEE

⅓ CUP (50G) UNSALTED ROASTED CASHEWS

2 TEASPOONS MUSTARD SEEDS

1 TEASPOON FENNEL SEEDS

¼ CUP FRESH CURRY LEAVES

1 Heat ghee in a large heavy-based saucepan over high heat, add onion, garlic and ginger; cook, stirring for 4 minutes, or until onion is golden brown. Add turmeric and garam masala; cook, stirring for 30 seconds or until fragrant.

2 Add lentils, tomato, chilli and the water; bring to the boil. Reduce heat; simmer, covered, for 15 minutes or until tender.

3 Add cauliflower and parsnip; simmer, covered, for 10 minutes or until cauliflower is just tender. Season.

4 Meanwhile, make cashew topping.

5 Add chard to dhal; simmer, covered, for 2 minutes or until just wilted.

6 Serve dhal topped with cashew topping and yoghurt, along with pappadums.

cashew topping Heat ghee in a small frying pan over medium heat, add nuts; cook, stirring for 2 minutes, or until golden and toasted. Stir in seeds and curry leaves; cook, stirring, for 1 minute or until leaves are crisp.

prep + cook time 40 minutes **serves** 4

nutritional count per serving 19.9g total fat (8.4g saturated fat); 2136kJ (510 cal); 46.5g carbohydrate; 26.5g protein; 21.6g fibre

tip Ghee is clarified butter, you can use butter or vegetable oil instead.

BEEF CURRY
With TURMERIC RICE

3 SHALLOTS (75G), CHOPPED

5 CLOVES GARLIC, CHOPPED

6 FRESH SMALL RED CHILLIES

30G (1-OUNCE) PIECE FRESH GINGER, CHOPPED FINELY

1 LEMON GRASS STALK, WHITE PART ONLY, SLICED THINLY

1 TABLESPOON TAMARIND PUREE

1 TABLESPOON COCONUT OIL

1KG (2 POUNDS) LEAN BEEF BOLAR BLADE ROAST OR BEEF SKIRT STEAK, CUT INTO 3CM (1¼-INCH) PIECES

1.5 LITRES (6 CUPS) WATER, APPROXIMATELY

½ CUP (140G) GREEK-STYLE YOGHURT

FRESH RED CHILLI, SLICED AND FRESH CORIANDER (CILANTRO) LEAVES, TO SERVE

TURMERIC RICE

1 TABLESPOON COCONUT OIL

1½ CUPS (300G) BASMATI RICE, RINSED

2 TEASPOONS MUSTARD SEEDS

½ TEASPOON GROUND TURMERIC

2 CUPS (500ML) CHICKEN STOCK

COCONUT SAMBAL

¼ CUP (10G) FLAKED COCONUT, TOASTED

1 LEBANESE CUCUMBER (130G), SEEDED, CHOPPED FINELY

1 SMALL RED ONION (100G), CHOPPED FINELY

1 TABLESPOON LIME JUICE

1 Process shallots, garlic, chilli, ginger, lemon grass and tamarind until smooth.

2 Heat coconut oil a large heavy-based saucepan over medium heat, add paste; cook, stirring for 3 minutes, or until fragrant.

3 Add beef to pan with enough of the water to completely cover beef; bring to the boil. Reduce heat; simmer, uncovered, for 2½ hours. Liquid will slowly evaporate and beef will become very tender. Add more water during cooking if necessary. Shred beef with two forks.

4 Make turmeric rice, then coconut sambal.

5 Serve curry topped with yoghurt, chilli and coriander, along with turmeric rice and coconut sambal.

turmeric rice Heat coconut oil in a medium saucepan over high heat, add rice, seeds and turmeric; cook, stirring, for 1 minute to coat rice well. Add stock; bring to the boil. Cover with a firm fitting lid; reduce heat to low, simmer for 12 minutes or until tunnels appear on surface of rice. Remove from heat; stand, covered, for 10 minutes. Fluff grains with a fork.

coconut sambal Combine ingredients in a small bowl.

prep + cook time 3 hours **serves** 4

nutritional count per serving 40g total fat (21.4g saturated fat); 4441kJ (1061 cal); 71.7g carbohydrate; 99.2g protein; 4.6g fibre

tip To save time buy ready made rendang paste, available from the Asian section of most supermarkets.

CAVOLO NERO *And* MUSHROOM LASAGNE

1KG (2 POUNDS) FRESH RICOTTA

1½ CUPS (120G) GRATED PECORINO CHEESE

1 CUP (250ML) BUTTERMILK

½ TEASPOON GROUND NUTMEG

1 TABLESPOON FINELY GRATED LEMON RIND

2 TABLESPOONS OLIVE OIL

2 CLOVES GARLIC, CRUSHED

4 GREEN ONIONS (SCALLIONS), SLICED THINLY

500G (1 POUND) SMALL PORTOBELLO MUSHROOMS, SLICED THINLY

400G (12½ OUNCES) CAVOLO NERO (TUSCAN CABBAGE), TRIMMED, CHOPPED

350G (11 OUNCES) FRESH WHOLEMEAL LASAGNE SHEETS

1 TABLESPOON OLIVE OIL, EXTRA

½ CUP (70G) HAZELNUTS, CHOPPED COARSELY

1 MEDIUM LEMON (140G), RIND CUT INTO THIN STRIPS

1 FRESH LONG GREEN CHILLI, SLICED THINLY

1 Combine ricotta, half the pecorino, the buttermilk, nutmeg and grated rind in a large bowl.

2 Heat oil in a large frying pan over medium-high heat, add garlic, half the green onion and 400g (12½ ounces) of the mushrooms; cook, covered, for 5 minutes or until mushrooms start to soften. Add 300g (9½ ounces) of the cavolo nero; stir until wilted. Cool slightly.

3 Preheat oven to 180°C/350°F.

4 Grease a 3-litre (12 cup) ovenproof dish. Spread base with ¼ cup of the ricotta mixture. Top with a single layer of lasagne sheets, trimming to fit. Top with one-third of the remaining ricotta mixture and half the mushroom mixture. Continue layering, ending with ricotta mixture.

5 Cover lasagne with foil. Bake for 25 minutes. Remove foil; bake a further 20 minutes or until pasta is cooked through and top is golden brown.

6 Meanwhile, heat extra oil in a medium frying pan over high heat; cook remaning mushrooms and remaning cavolo nero, stirring, for 3 minutes. Add remaining green onion, the hazelnuts, rind strips and chilli; toss to combine.

7 Serve lasagne topped with mushroom mixture and remaining pecorino.

prep + cook time 1 hour 30 minutes **serves** 6
nutritional count per serving 43.1g total fat (18g saturated fat); 3084kJ (737 cal); 43.7g carbohydrate; 38.2g protein; 11.4g fibre
tip Lasagne can be made a day ahead. Keep, covered, in the refrigerator.

FISHERMAN'S SOUP
WITH TURMERIC ROUILLE

1 TABLESPOON OLIVE OIL

1 MEDIUM BROWN ONION (150G), SLICED THICKLY

2 CLOVES GARLIC, SLICED THINLY

2 BABY FENNEL BULBS (260G), SLICED THINLY, FRONDS RESERVED

1 FRESH LONG RED CHILLI, SLICED THINLY

PINCH SAFFRON THREADS

1 BAY LEAF

2 CUPS (500ML) SALT-REDUCED VEGETABLE STOCK

2 CUPS (500ML) WATER

400G (12½ OUNCES) CANNED CHERRY TOMATOES

2 BLUE SWIMMER CRABS (860G), QUARTERED, CLEANED

300G (9½ OUNCES) FIRM WHITE FISH FILLET, CUT INTO 4CM (1½-INCH) PIECES

8 LARGE UNCOOKED PRAWNS (SHRIMP) (500G), PEELED AND DEVEINED, TAILS INTACT

2 MEDIUM CALAMARI (320G), CLEANED, SLICED, LEGS RESERVED

TURMERIC ROUILLE

2 FREE-RANGE EGG YOLKS

1 CLOVE GARLIC, CHOPPED COARSELY

2 TEASPOONS WHITE BALSAMIC VINEGAR

1 TEASPOON DIJON MUSTARD

½ TEASPOON FINELY GRATED FRESH TURMERIC

⅓ CUP (80ML) OLIVE OIL

⅔ CUP (160ML) MACADAMIA OIL

1 Heat oil in large saucepan over medium-high heat; cook onion, garlic and fennel, stirring, for 5 minutes or until soft. Add chilli, saffron and bay leaf; cook, stirring for 2 minutes or until fragrant. Add stock, the water and tomatoes; bring to the boil. Reduce heat; simmer, covered, for 30 minutes.

2 Meanwhile, make turmeric rouille.

3 Add crab, fish, prawns and calamari to pan; cook, covered, for 8 minutes or until seafood is just cooked.

4 Serve soup topped with reserved fennel fronds, along with rouille.

turmeric rouille Process yolks, garlic, vinegar, mustard and turmeric in a small food processor until smooth. Gradually add combined oils in a thin stream until mixture is thick. Season.

prep + cook time 1 hour serves 4

nutritional count per serving 65.2g total fat (10.1g saturated fat); 3473kJ (829 cal); 7.3g carbohydrate; 53.2g protein; 3.4g fibre

tip Use a tiny pinch of saffron powder instead of threads, if you like.

I AM

DAIRY FREE

PROTEIN RICH

LOW CARB

BLACK RICE
SEAFOOD PAELLA

¼ CUP (60ML) OLIVE OIL

1 MEDIUM WHITE ONION (150G), CHOPPED FINELY

1½ TEASPOONS SMOKED PAPRIKA

1 SMALL RED CAPSICUM (BELL PEPPER) (150G), SLICED THICKLY

2 CLOVES GARLIC, CHOPPED

1 CUP (200G) BLACK RICE, RINSED

400G (12½ OUNCES) CANNED CHERRY TOMATOES

2 CUPS (500ML) VEGETABLE STOCK

2 CUPS (500ML) WATER

8 LARGE UNCOOKED PRAWNS (SHRIMP) (500G), PEELED AND DEVEINED, TAILS INTACT

300G (9½ OUNCES) FIRM WHITE FISH FILLETS, CUT INTO 4CM (1½-INCH) PIECES

4 SCALLOPS ON SHELL (100G)

8 PIPIS (320G)

½ CUP (60G) FROZEN PEAS

¼ CUP FRESH FLAT-LEAF PARSLEY LEAVES

LEMON WEDGES, TO SERVE

1 Heat oil in a large frying pan or paella pan over medium heat.; cook onion, stirring, for 3 minutes or until softened. Add paprika, capsicum, garlic and rice; cook, stirring, for 2 minutes or until well combined. Add tomatoes, stock and the water; bring to the boil. Reduce heat; simmer, uncovered, stirring occasionally, for 40 minutes or until most of the liquid has been absorbed and rice is tender.

2 Arrange seafood and peas on rice mixture; season. Cook, covered, for 5 minutes or until seafood is just cooked through.

3 Serve paella topped with parsley and lemon wedges.

prep + cook time 1 hour **serves** 4

nutritional count per serving 17.4g total fat (3g saturated fat); 2202kJ (526 cal); 45.6g carbohydrate; 42.5g protein; 6.9g fibre

tip Recipe is best made just before serving.

SUPER SWEETS

THE GOOD NEWS IS, WHEN IT COMES TO NUTRITIONALLY BENEFICIAL FOODS, YOU CAN STILL HAVE DESSERT. TREATS CONTAINING BERRIES, CITRUS, COCONUT, YOGHURT, NUTS AND CACAO ARE PACKED WITH HEALTHY GOODNESS.

TO UNMOULD PANNA COTTA, RUB THE OUTSIDE OF THE MOULD WITH A HOT KITCHEN CLOTH. HOLD THE MOULD UPSIDE DOWN IN YOUR CUPPED HAND, THEN SHAKE IT GENTLY UNTIL PANNA COTTA RELEASES FROM THE MOULD; CAREFULLY TRANSFER TO A SERVING PLATE.

CHAMOMILE *And* BUTTERMILK
PANNA COTTA

1 CUP (250ML) MILK

¼ CUP (50G) NORBU (MONK FRUIT SUGAR)

8 CHAMOMILE TEA BAGS

2 TEASPOONS POWDERED GELATINE

2 TABLESPOONS WATER

1 CUP (250M) BUTTERMILK

1 MEDIUM LEMON (140G), SLICED THINLY

¼ CUP (90G) HONEY, WARMED

1 TABLESPOON LEMON JUICE

2 TABLESPOONS ALMOND KERNELS, TOASTED, CHOPPED COARSELY

1 Place milk, norbu and tea bags in a medium saucepan over low heat, stirring, for 2 minutes or until sugar dissolves and mixture comes almost to the boil. Remove from heat. Press tea bags against the side of the pan to extract flavour, add back to the mixture; stand for 10 minutes. Strain mixture; discard tea bags.

2 Sprinkle gelatine over the water in a small heatproof jug; stand jug in a small saucepan of simmering water. Stir mixture until gelatine dissolves; cool for 5 minutes. Add gelatine mixture and buttermilk to milk mixture; stir until combined.

3 Rinse four ⅔ cup (160ml) moulds with cold water, do not dry; place on an oven tray. Pour panna cotta mixture into moulds. Refrigerate 6 hours or overnight until set.

4 Preheat oven to 220°C/425°F. Grease a large oven tray; line with baking paper.

5 Place lemon slices, in a single layer, on tray; drizzle with honey and juice. Roast for 10 minutes, turning over halfway through cooking and basting occasionally with juices on tray until caramelised.

6 Serve panna cotta topped with lemon slices, almonds and any juices on the oven tray.

prep + cook time 30 minutes (+ refrigeration) **serves** 4
nutritional count per serving 7.1g total fat (2.4g saturated fat); 866kJ (207 cal); 26.8g carbohydrate; 7.8g protein; 1.1g fibre
tip You can use other types of tea in this recipe such as peppermint or earl grey, if you like.

I AM

VEGAN

SUGAR FREE

RAW

SUGAR-FREE CHOCOLATE IS AVAILABLE FROM HEALTH
FOOD STORES AND PHARMACIES. USE LIME INSTEAD OF LEMON.
THIS TERRINE CAN BE MADE 2 WEEKS AHEAD.

COCONUT *And* CHOC NUT
FROZEN TERRINE

You will need to soak the cashews for 3 hours first before you can continue with the recipe.

2½ CUPS (375G) RAW CASHEWS

1 CUP (80G) DESICCATED COCONUT

½ CUP (120G) COCONUT OIL, AT ROOM TEMPERATURE

1 TABLESPOON FINELY GRATED LEMON RIND

½ CUP (125ML) LEMON JUICE

⅓ CUP (80ML) PURE MAPLE SYRUP

1 CUP (120G) PECANS

⅓ CUP (35G) GROUND HAZELNUTS

¼ CUP (60G) COCONUT OIL, EXTRA

50G (1½ OUNCES) SUGAR-FREE DARK CHOCOLATE, CHOPPED COARSELY

2 TABLESPOON PURE MAPLE SYRUP, EXTRA

125G (4 OUNCES) BLUEBERRIES

½ CUP (25G) FLAKED COCONUT, TOASTED

1 Soak cashews in cold water for 3 hours. Drain.

2 Grease and line the base and sides of a 9cm x 19.5cm (3¾-inch x 8-inch) loaf pan with baking paper, extending the paper 5cm (2 inches) above the edge.

3 Process drained cashews with desiccated coconut, coconut oil, rind, juice and maple syrup until smooth. Spoon cashew mixture into pan, pushing the mixture into the corners; smooth the surface. Freeze for 2 hours or until set.

4 Place pecans, ground hazelnuts, extra coconut oil, chocolate and half the extra maple syrup in the food processor; process until mixture is finely chopped.

5 Spread pecan mixture on cashew mixture to completely cover. Return to freezer for 1 hour or until firm.

6 Remove from freezer; stand at room temperature for 10 minutes before inverting onto a serving plate. Serve topped with blueberries and flaked coconut, drizzled with remaining extra maple syrup.

prep + cook time 30 minutes (+ soaking & freezing)
serves 8
nutritional count per serving 67.9g total fat (32.7g saturated fat); 3209kJ (766 cal); 24.9g carbohydrate; 11.4g protein; 7.2g fibre

THIS PUDDING WOULD ALSO BE DELICIOUS SERVED
WITH SLICED MANGO INSTEAD OF PAPAYA.

COCONUT RED RICE PUDDING
WITH PAPAYA And LIME

¾ CUP (150G) RED RICE, RINSED

2 CUPS (500ML) COCONUT MILK

¼ CUP (70G) COARSELY GRATED PALM SUGAR

2 TABLESPOONS COCONUT CREAM

½ MEDIUM PAPAYA (500G), SLICED

½ CUP (25G) FLAKED COCONUT, TOASTED

1 LIME, CUT INTO CHEEKS

1 Cook rice in a small saucepan of boiling water for 30 minutes or until almost tender; drain.

2 Return rice to pan with coconut milk and sugar; bring to the boil. Cook, stirring occasionally, for 15 minutes or until rice is tender and liquid has thickened slightly.

3 Spoon rice into serving bowls, top with coconut cream, papaya and flaked coconut. Serve pudding with lime cheeks.

prep + cook time 50 minutes **serves** 4
nutritional count per serving 29.9g total fat (25.9g saturated fat); 1811kJ (432 cal); 35.5g carbohydrate; 4.7g protein; 5.4g fibre

I AM
VITAMIN RICH
HIGH IN FOLATE
LOW FAT

PINEAPPLE *And* MELON
GRANITA

1 STICK FRESH LEMON GRASS, WHITE PART ONLY, BRUISED

½ CUP (135G) COARSELY GRATED PALM SUGAR

⅔ CUP (160ML) WATER

½ SMALL PINEAPPLE (600G), PEELED, CHOPPED COARSELY

2 TEASPOONS FINELY GRATED LIME RIND

2 TABLESPOONS LIME JUICE

¾ CUP (200G) GREEK-STYLE YOGHURT

½ MEDIUM PAPAYA (500G), PEELED, SLICED THICKLY

½ SMALL ROCKMELON (650G), PEELED, SLICED THICKLY

¼ CUP SMALL FRESH MINT LEAVES

1 Place lemon grass, sugar and the water in a medium saucepan; cook, stirring, over low heat until sugar dissolves. Bring to the boil; remove from heat. Pour syrup into a large heatproof jug or bowl; cool.

2 Meanwhile, blend or process pineapple until smooth; you will need 1½ cups pulp. Whisk pineapple, rind, juice and yoghurt into cooled syrup. Pour pineapple mixture into a 20cm x 30cm (8-inch x 12-inch) (base measurement) metal slice pan. Freeze for 3 hours or until just beginning to freeze. Using a fork, scrape the mixture to break up ice crystals. Cover; freeze for 4 hours, scraping the mixture every hour, or until completely frozen.

3 Serve granita with papaya, rockmelon and mint.

prep + cook time 40 minutes (+ cooling & freezing)

serves 4

nutritional count per serving 3.3g total fat (1.9g saturated fat); 1185kJ (283 cal); 57.2g carbohydrate; 4.4g protein; 5g fibre

tip Use vanilla-flavoured yoghurt instead of greek-style yoghurt, if you like.

CHOC FUDGE
With MACADAMIA MILK ICE-CREAM

3¼ CUPS (810ML) MACADAMIA MILK

1 CUP (220G) MAPLE SUGAR

2 TEASPOONS VANILLA BEAN PASTE

100G (3 OUNCES) SUGAR-FREE MILK CHOCOLATE, CHOPPED COARSELY

1 TEASPOON COCONUT OIL

CHOC FUDGE

2 CUPS (320G) BLANCHED ALMONDS

2 CUPS (160G) DESICCATED COCONUT

200G (6½ OUNCES) MEDJOOL PITTED DATES, CHOPPED COARSELY

½ CUP (50G) COCOA POWDER

2 TEASPOONS SALT FLAKES

¼ CUP (60ML) PURE MAPLE SYRUP

50G (1½ OUNCES) COCOA BUTTER, MELTED

2 TABLESPOONS MACADAMIAS, ROASTED, CHOPPED COARSELY

1 Stir macadamia milk and maple sugar in a medium saucepan over medium heat for 2 minutes or until sugar dissolves. Stir in paste. Transfer to a heatproof bowl. Refrigerate until cold.

2 Pour chilled ice-cream mixture into an ice-cream machine. Churn, follow manufactures instructions. Transfer to freezer.

3 Meanwhile, make choc fudge. Cut fudge into 2.5cm x 10cm (1-inch x 4-inch) pieces.

4 Place chocolate and coconut oil in a microwave-safe bowl. Microwave on HIGH (100%) in 30-second bursts until melted and smooth.

5 Serve scoops of ice-cream with fudge, drizzled with chocolate and sprinkled with macadamias.

choc fudge Grease and line a 20cm (8-inch) square cake pan with baking paper. Process almonds until finely ground. Add coconut and dates, process until mixture forms a soft paste. Add cocoa, salt, maple syrup and cocoa butter; process until smooth. Press mixture into pan. Refrigerate until firm.

prep + cook time 30 minutes (+ refrigeration & freezing)
serves 6
nutritional count per serving 78g total fat (29.3g saturated fat); 4711kJ (1125 cal); 89.1g carbohydrate; 21.8g protein; 17.8g fibre
tip Ice-cream and fudge can be made up to 1 week ahead.

I AM

GLUTEN FREE

LACTOSE FREE

VITAMIN E

I AM
PROTEIN RICH
HIGH IN CALCIUM
VITAMIN A

BAKED RICOTTA PUDDINGS
with ORANGE and DATE SALAD

1 MEDIUM ORANGE (240G)

1 MEDIUM BLOOD ORANGE (240G)

600G (1¼ POUNDS) RICOTTA

3 FREE-RANGE EGGS

⅓ CUP (80ML) PURE MAPLE SYRUP

½ TEASPOON GROUND CINNAMON

4 FRESH DATES (80G), SEEDED, TORN

2 TABLESPOONS PINE NUTS, TOASTED

THYME SPRIGS, TO SERVE

ORANGE SYRUP

½ CUP (125ML) FRESHLY SQUEEZED ORANGE JUICE

2 TABLESPOONS PURE MAPLE SYRUP

1 CINNAMON STICK

½ TEASPOON FRESH THYME LEAVES

1 Preheat oven to 180°C/350°F. Grease four ¾ cup (180ml), 10cm (4-inch) ovenproof dishes.

2 Finely grate rind from orange; you need 2 teaspoons. Cut the top and bottom from orange and blood orange; cut off the white pith, following the curve of the fruit. Holding the orange, cut down both sides of the white membrane to release each segment. Cut blood orange into thick slices. Set aside.

3 Process ricotta, eggs, syrup, cinnamon and rind until smooth. Pour mixture evenly into dishes.

4 Bake puddings for 20 minutes or until centre is just firm to touch. Cool to room temperature. Refrigerate for at least 1 hour or until cold.

5 Meanwhile, make orange syrup.

6 Serve puddings topped with orange segments, dates, syrup, pine nuts and thyme.

orange syrup Bring ingredients to the boil in a small saucepan. Reduce heat to low; simmer 10 minutes or until syrupy. Refrigerate for 1 hour or until cold. Remove cinnamon stick.

prep + cook time 1 hour (+ cooling & refrigeration)
serves 4
nutritional count per serving 25.7g total fat (12.3g saturated fat); 2201kJ (526 cal); 49.9g carbohydrate; 23.1g protein; 5g fibre

MILD-FLAVOURED

Try floral yellow box, macadamia (from hives placed on macadamia tree plantations) and meadow honey from South Australia in dairy-based desserts, or recipes where a non-assertive flavour is best.

MEDIUM-FLAVOURED

Leatherwood is a full-bodied and spiced honey from Tasmania, while blue gum honey comes from a variety of regions, both add a wonderful taste to baked goods or use raw for a defined honey taste in both sweet and savoury recipes.

FULL FLAVOURED

Eucalypt honeys are generally more assertive in taste with toffee and smoky flavours; try red stringy bark one of the lowest GI rated honeys (44) or antioxidant-rich red gum in dressings or marinades for meat.

MEDICINAL HONEY

Manuka honey is produced from the nectar of wild-growing tea tree bush in New Zealand and south east Australia and is famed for its exceptional anti-bacterial properties, leading to its use as a dressing for wounds and in ointments.

HONEY FACTS

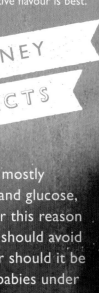

Honey is mostly fructose and glucose, and so for this reason diabetics should avoid it and nor should it be given to babies under one. While honey is, well sugar, and all sugar should be consumed in moderation, it also contains some goodies. One of which is amylase, an enzyme that helps the digestive system break down starch. Others are propolis the material that bees use to build their hives, which has anti-microbial, anti-fungal and anti-bacterial properties as well as antioxidants, but all of these are destroyed when heated. Raw floral honeys have a low GI, while cheaper blended honeys tend to be high GI.

Commercial honey

Most commercial honey is a blend of floral sources, from different geographical locations. The honey is usually heated to liquefy microcrystals and make it free-flowing, then filtered, processes that can remove much of the health benefits. This type of honey is clear, honey-coloured and with few if any noticeable flavour notes.

HONEY IS HYGROSCOPIC, MEANING IT ATTRACTS MOISTURE, KEEPING BAKED GOODS MOIST. WHILE THE NUTRITIONAL BENEFITS OF RAW HONEY ARE LOST IN COOKING, THERE ARE STILL BENEFITS IN TASTE.

A SINGLE WORKER BEE WILL COLLECT ONLY *half a teaspoon* OF HONEY IN ITS SIX-WEEK LIFE SPAN.

HONEY

NON

REFINED

SUGAR

OF ALL THE SWEETENERS *Honey* IS ONE OF THE MOST NATURAL, IF IT IS CHOSEN WISELY. HONEY IS CLASSIFIED BY THE *floral source* OF THE *nectar*, WHICH DETERMINES TASTE. IT CAN BE FROM A SINGLE SOURCE OR IT CAN BE A BLEND OF DIFFERENT ONES.

UPSIDE DOWN
GRAPE *And* HONEY CAKE

8CM (3¼-INCH) ROSEMARY SPRIG

250G (8 OUNCES) SMALL RED SEEDLESS GRAPES, HALVED

½ CUP (180G) HONEY

4 FREE-RANGE EGGS

½ CUP (125ML) EXTRA VIRGIN OLIVE OIL

⅓ CUP (95G) GREEK-STYLE YOGHURT

1 TEASPOON FINELY GRATED LEMON RIND

1 CUP (150G) PLAIN (ALL-PURPOSE) FLOUR

⅔ CUP (100G) PLAIN (ALL-PURPOSE) WHOLEMEAL FLOUR

2 TEASPOONS BAKING POWDER

1 CUP (280G) GREEK-STYLE YOGHURT, EXTRA

RED WINE VINEGAR SYRUP

½ CUP (125ML) RED WINE VINEGAR

¾ CUP (270G) HONEY

1 Preheat oven to 140°C/280°F fan-forced. Grease and line base and side of a 22cm (8¾-inch) round cake pan, extending the paper 5cm (2 inches) above the edge.

2 Make red wine vinegar syrup; pour into pan to cover the base. Cool 5 minutes.

3 Place rosemary sprig in the centre of the syrup. Taking care as the syrup will still be hot, arrange grape halves snugly, cut-side up, in concentric circles starting from the outside of the pan, until syrup is covered.

4 Beat honey and eggs in a large bowl with an electric mixer on high speed for 8 minutes or until almost tripled in volume. With the motor operating, gradually add oil, then yoghurt and rind, beating briefly just to combine.

5 Sift flours and baking powder over egg mixture, return husks to bowl. Using a balloon whisk, gently stir dry mixture into egg mixture, taking care not to deflate the mixture. Pour mixture into pan; level surface.

6 Bake cake, on the lowest shelf, for 1 hour 10 minutes or until a skewer inserted into the centre comes out clean. Stand in pan for 15 minutes.

7 Cut back the paper collar, then using a tea towel or oven mitts, invert the hot cake onto a serving plate. Cool completely. Serve cake with extra yoghurt.

red wine vinegar syrup Bring ingredients to the boil in a medium saucepan over medium heat, stirring, until well combined. Boil rapidly for 5 minutes or until syrupy and reduced to ½ cup (125ml).

prep + cook time 1 hour 30 minutes (+ standing)
serves 8
nutritional count per serving 19.9g total fat (4.9g saturated fat); 2424kJ (579 cal); 91.1g carbohydrate; 9.5g protein; 2.9g fibre
tip This cake is best made on day of serving.

I AM

SUGAR FREE

ANTIOXIDANTS

LOW FAT

ALMOND SPREAD IS AVAILABLE AT HEALTH FOOD STORES AND MOST SUPERMARKETS. TO MAKE YOUR OWN, BLEND OR PROCESS WHOLE ROASTED ALMONDS TO A FINE PASTE, ADDING SALT AND MAPLE SYRUP TO TASTE.

RHUBARB & BERRY CRUMBLES
WITH RICOTTA CREAM

250G (8 OUNCES) RHUBARB, TRIMMED, CUT INTO 4CM (1½-INCH) LENGTHS

2 TABLESPOONS FRESHLY SQUEEZED ORANGE JUICE

1 TABLESPOON HONEY

250G (8 OUNCES) MIXED FROZEN BERRIES, HALVE STRAWBERRIES IF LARGE

2 TABLESPOONS TRADITIONAL ROLLED OATS

2 TABLESPOONS QUINOA FLAKES

2 TABLESPOONS LIGHT BROWN SUGAR

¼ CUP (70G) ALMOND SPREAD

RICOTTA CREAM

½ CUP (120G) FRESH RICOTTA

2 TABLESPOONS MILK

2 TEASPOONS HONEY

1 TEASPOON FINELY GRATED ORANGE RIND

1 Preheat oven to 180°C/350°F.

2 Combine rhubarb, juice and honey in a small saucepan; stand for 10 minutes.

3 Bring rhubarb mixture to a simmer; cook, covered, for 2 minutes, or until just starting to soften. Stir in berries. Spoon mixture into four ¾-cup (180ml) ovenproof dishes. Place dishes on an oven tray.

4 Combine oats, quinoa and sugar in a small bowl. Rub in almond spread until mixture resembles coarse crumbs. Sprinkle mixture evenly on fruit.

5 Bake crumbles for 20 minutes or until topping is crisp and golden.

6 Meanwhile, make ricotta cream.

7 Serve crumbles warm with ricotta cream.

ricotta cream Blend or process ingredients until smooth.

prep + cook time 40 minutes serves 4

nutritional count per serving 14g total fat (3.1g saturated fat); 1203kJ (287 cal); 28.3g carbohydrate; 9.8g protein; 6.1g fibre

KEEP THE UNUSED COCONUT LIQUID FROM THE CANS OF COCONUT CREAM FOR ANOTHER USE. ASSEMBLE FRUIT STACKS ON THE DAY OF SERVING.

PURE GOODNESS
FRUIT STACKS

You will need to refrigerate the cans of coconut cream overnight first before you can continue with the recipe.

1 MEDIUM ROCKMELON (1.7KG), HALVED CROSSWAYS, PEELED, SEEDED

1 MEDIUM HONEYDEW (1.5KG), HALVED CROSSWAYS, PEELED, SEEDED

½ WHOLE SEEDLESS WATERMELON (2.25KG), RIND REMOVED

1 MEDIUM FIGS (60G), CUT INTO SIX WEDGES

1 FINGER LIME (60G), HALVED LENGTHWAYS, PULP RESERVED

¼ CUP (30G) FINELY CHOPPED PISTACHIOS

WHIPPED COCONUT CREAM

2 X 400ML CANS COCONUT CREAM

1 Make whipped coconut cream.

2 Cut rockmelon, honeydew and watermelon crossways into 4cm (1½-inch) thick slices. Using a 4.5cm (1¾-inch) round cutter, cut rounds from fruit slices; you should get 6 rounds from each fruit.

3 Top each fruit round with whipped coconut cream. Stack three rounds together. Top fruit stacks with fig wedge, finger lime pulp and pistachios. Refrigerate until ready to serve.

whipped coconut cream Refrigerate cans of coconut cream standing upright overnight. Carefully remove lid, scoop the solid top from coconut cream into a small bowl of an electric mixer. Reserve remaining liquid in can for another use. Beat coconut cream until medium peaks form.

prep time 30 minutes (+ refrigeration) **makes** 6
nutritional count per stack 12.4g total fat (8g saturated fat); 1335kJ (319 cal); 43.2g carbohydrate; 5.5g protein; 7.6g fibre

I AM

DAIRY FREE
MINERAL RICH

VEGAN

I AM

HIGH FIBRE

PROTEIN RICH

VITAMIN B

PEAR & CHOCOLATE
RYE BREAD PUDDING

300G (9½-OUNCE) LOAF RYE BREAD, TORN INTO PIECES

8 SMALL PARADISE PEARS (450G), UNPEELED, HALVED, QUARTERED AND SOME LEFT WHOLE

40G (1½ OUNCES) BUTTER, SOFTENED

100G (3 OUNCES) DARK CHOCOLATE (70% COCOA), CHOPPED COARSELY

2 CUPS (500ML) MILK

300ML POURING CREAM

¼ CUP (60ML) PURE MAPLE SYRUP

¾ TEASPOON GROUND CINNAMON

PINCH OF SALT

3 FREE-RANGE EGGS

2 TABLESPOON PURE MAPLE SYRUP, EXTRA

1 Preheat oven to 160°C/325°F. Grease a shallow 2-litre (8-cup) ovenproof dish.

2 Place torn bread and pear in dish, dot with butter then scatter with chocolate.

3 Bring milk, cream, maple syrup, cinnamon and salt to the boil in a medium saucepan. Whisk eggs in a large heatproof bowl. Gradually whisk hot milk mixture into egg. Pour mixture over bread mixture.

4 Bake pudding for 50 minutes or until just set. Stand for 5 minutes before serving, drizzled with extra maple syrup.

prep + cook time 1 hour 30 minutes **serves** 4
nutritional count per serving 52.1g total fat (29.4g saturated fat); 3857kJ (921 cal); 94g carbohydrate; 19.4g protein; 7.2g fibre

RED COLOURED FRUITS LIKE STRAWBERRIES, GRAPES AND CHERRIES ARE HIGH IN ANTIOXIDANTS.

RED FRUIT SALAD
with CHAI SPICED YOGHURT

½ CUP (125ML) WATER

2 TABLESPOONS HONEY

1 CINNAMON STICK

3CM (1¼-INCH) PIECE FRESH GINGER, CUT INTO THIN MATCHSTICKS

2 CARDAMOM PODS, BRUISED

2 WHOLE CLOVES

1 WHOLE STAR ANISE

500G (1-POUND) PIECE WATERMELON, RIND REMOVED, CUT INTO SMALL WEDGES

250G (8 OUNCES) STRAWBERRIES, HALVED

250G (8 OUNCES) RED SEEDLESS GRAPES, HALVED

250G (8 OUNCES) CHERRIES, HALVED, SEEDS REMOVED

1½ CUPS (420G) GREEK-STYLE YOGHURT

¼ CUP (30G) SLIVERED PISTACHIOS

MICRO HERBS, TO SERVE (OPTIONAL)

1 Stir the water, honey, cinnamon, ginger, cardamom, cloves and star anise in a small saucepan over medium heat until honey dissolves. Bring to the boil. Reduce heat; simmer, uncovered, for 2 minutes until liquid reduces by half. Remove from heat; cool completely.

2 Combine watermelon, strawberries, grapes and cherries in a bowl; drizzle with half the cooled syrup. Refrigerate for 10 minutes.

3 Stir remaining syrup through yoghurt.

4 Serve fruit salad topped with pistachios and micro herbs, along with the yogurt mixture.

prep + cook time 15 minutes (+ cooling & refrigeration)

serves 4

nutritional count per serving 10.5g total fat (4.5g saturated fat); 1450kJ (346 cal); 51.3g carbohydrate; 9.2g protein; 4.8g fibre

I AM

POTASSIUM

ANTIOXIDANTS

LOW GI

I AM

GLUTEN FREE
ANTIOXIDANTS
HIGH FIBRE

UNICED CAKES CAN BE MADE 2 DAYS AHEAD. STORE IN
AN AIRTIGHT CONTAINER. ICE CAKES ON DAY OF SERVING.

FLOURLESS CHOCOLATE CAKES
With AVOCADO ICING

3 FREE-RANGE EGGS, SEPARATED

⅔ CUP (150G) CASTER (SUPERFINE) SUGAR

1 TEASPOON VANILLA EXTRACT

75G (2½ OUNCES) DARK CHOCOLATE (70% COCOA), GRATED FINELY

¾ CUP (75G) GROUND HAZELNUTS

¼ CUP (60G) COCONUT OIL, MELTED

125G (4 OUNCES) RASPBERRIES

AVOCADO ICING

1 LARGE RIPE AVOCADO (320G)

2 TABLESPOONS COCOA POWDER

2 TABLESPOONS COCONUT OIL, MELTED

2 TABLESPOONS AGAVE NECTAR

1 Preheat oven to 180°C/350°F. Grease six ¾ cup (180ml) friand pans; line bases and sides with baking paper.

2 Beat egg yolks, ½ cup (110g) of the sugar and the extract with an electric mixer until thick and pale. Fold in combined chocolate and ground hazelnuts.

3 Beat egg whites in a small bowl with electric mixer until soft peaks form. Gradually add remaining sugar; beat until sugar dissolves between additions and mixture is glossy and stiff. Gently fold egg white mixture into egg yolk mixture with coconut oil. Pour into pans.

4 Bake cakes for 20 minutes or until a skewer inserted in centre comes out clean. Leave in pans for 10 minutes; turn, top-side up, onto a wire rack to cool.

5 Make avocado icing.

6 Spread icing onto cooled cakes; top with raspberries.

avocado icing Blend or process ingredients until smooth and glossy.

prep + cook time 45 minutes (+ cooling) **makes** 6
nutritional count per cake 38.8g total fat (20.8g saturated fat); 2245kJ (536 cal); 41.3g carbohydrate; 7.2g protein; 4.4g fibre

YOU WILL NEED ABOUT 2 PASSIONFRUIT FOR THIS RECIPE. USE COCONUT YOGHURT INSTEAD OF GREEK-STYLE YOGHURT, IF YOU PREFER, AND OMIT THE BROWN SUGAR AND DESICCATED COCONUT.

NO-BAKE
BANANA COCONUT PIE

1 CUP (160G) BRAZIL NUTS

180G (5½ OUNCES) FRESH DATES, PITTED

½ CUP (45G) TRADITIONAL ROLLED OATS

½ CUP (40G) SHREDDED COCONUT

3 TEASPOONS POWDERED GELATINE

¼ CUP (60ML) BOILING WATER

3 CUPS (840G) GREEK-STYLE YOGHURT, AT ROOM TEMPERATURE

¼ CUP (55G) FIRMLY PACKED LIGHT BROWN SUGAR

¼ CUP (20G) FINE DESICCATED COCONUT

2 TEASPOONS FINELY GRATED LIME RIND

2 MEDIUM BANANAS (400G), SLICED

1 TABLESPOON LIME JUICE

2 TABLESPOONS PASSIONFRUIT PULP

¼ CUP (10G) FLAKED COCONUT, TOASTED

1 Lightly grease a 23cm (9¼-inch) round, 3cm (1¼-inch) deep, fluted flan tin with a removable base.

2 Process brazil nuts, dates, oats and shredded coconut until mixture forms a coarse paste. Press mixture evenly over base and side of tin.

3 Sprinkle gelatine over the just boiled water; whisk to dissolve, making sure there no lumps. Stir into yoghurt with sugar, desiccated coconut and rind. Pour mixture into pie shell. Cover; refrigerate for 4 hours or until set.

4 Gently toss banana slices in lime juice. Serve tart topped with banana, passionfruit and flaked coconut.

prep time 30 minutes (+ refrigeration) **serves** 8
nutritional count per serving 25.8g total fat (11.7g saturated fat); 1997kJ (477 cal); 46.9g carbohydrate; 11.5g protein; 7.1g fibre

TO·DAYS PRICE 4/- per lb.

RAW
BROWNIES

DATE & RASPBERRY

prep time 20 minutes (+ refrigeration) **makes** 25

Grease and line base and sides of a 20cm (8-in) square cake pan with baking paper. Process 2¼ cups (270g) pecans until finely chopped. With motor operating, add 2¼ cups (520g) fresh seeded dates, ⅓ cup raw cacao powder, 3 teaspoons water and 1½ teaspoons coconut oil; process until mixture comes together. Press mixture evenly into pan; level with a palette knife. Refrigerate for 1 hour or until firm. Drizzle with 50g (1½oz) melted 70% dark chocolate; top with 60g (2oz) raspberries. Cut into 25 squares.

CRUNCHY WALNUT

prep time 20 minutes (+ refrigeration) **makes** 25

Grease and line base and sides of a 20cm (8-in) square cake pan with baking paper. Process 2¼ cups (270g) pecans until finely chopped. With motor operating, add 2¼ cups (520g) fresh seeded dates, ⅓ cup (35g) raw cacao powder, 3 teaspoons water, 1½ teaspoons coconut oil and 1 teaspoon ground cinnamon; process until mixture comes together. Transfer to a bowl; stir in ½ cup (55g) chopped walnuts and ¼ cup (40g) cacao nibs. Press mixture evenly into pan; level with a palette knife. Refrigerate for 1 hour or until firm. Dust with 1 teaspoon cocoa powder. Cut into 25 squares.

PEANUT BUTTER & SEEDS

prep time 20 minutes (+ refrigeration) **makes** 25

Grease and line base and sides of a 20cm (8-in) square cake pan with baking paper. Combine 2 tablespoons sesame seeds, 1 tablespoon linseeds and ⅓ cup (65g) pepitas in a small bowl. Process 2¼ cups (270g) pecans until finely chopped. With motor operating, add 2¼ cups (520g) fresh seeded dates, ⅓ cup (35g) raw cacao powder, 3 teaspoons water and 1½ teaspoons coconut oil; process until mixture comes together. Transfer to a bowl; stir in half the seed mixture. Press half the mixture into pan; top with ½ cup (140g) natural peanut butter, in teaspoonfuls. Press on remaining date mixture. Refrigerate for 1 hour or until firm. Spread top with an extra ½ cup (140g) natural peanut butter; sprinkle with remaining seed mixture. Refrigerate for 30 minutes or until firm. Cut into 25 squares.

CITRUS & PISTACHIO

prep time 20 minutes (+ refrigeration) **makes** 25

Grease and line base and sides of a 20cm (8-in) square cake pan with baking paper. Process 2¼ cups (270g) pecans until finely chopped. With motor operating, add 2¼ cups (520g) fresh seeded dates, ⅓ cup (35g) raw cacao powder, 3 teaspoons water, 1½ teaspoons coconut oil, 2 teaspoons finely grated orange rind and 2 teaspoons finely grated lemon rind; process until mixture comes together. Transfer to a bowl; stir in ½ cup (70g) chopped pistachios. Press mixture evenly into pan; press on ½ cup (70g) chopped pistachios. Refrigerate for 1 hour or until firm. Cut into 25 squares.

I AM
HIGH FIBRE
HIGH IN FOLATE
DAIRY FREE

YOU WILL NEED 2 BUNCHES (1KG) BABY GOLDEN BEETROOT FOR THIS RECIPE: 1 BUNCH TO GET 1 CUP GRATED AMOUNT, AND 1 BUNCH FOR THE CANDIED BEETROOT.

GOLDEN BEETROOT And CARROT CAKES

3 CUPS (300G) GROUND HAZELNUTS

3 TEASPOONS BAKING POWDER

⅓ CUP (55G) SULTANAS

⅓ CUP (45G) COARSELY CHOPPED ROASTED HAZELNUTS

⅓ CUP (120G) HONEY

¼ CUP (60G) COCONUT OIL

1 TEASPOON VANILLA EXTRACT

1 TEASPOON MIXED SPICE

3 FREE-RANGE EGGS

1½ CUPS (175G) COARSELY GRATED CARROT

1 CUP (50G) COARSELY GRATED GOLDEN BEETROOT (BEETS)

VANILLA YOGHURT, TO SERVE (OPTIONAL)

CANDIED BEETROOT

1 BUNCH BABY GOLDEN BEETROOT (BEETS) (500G), SCRUBBED AND TRIMMED

1½ CUP (375ML) PURE MAPLE SYRUP

1 Preheat oven to 180°C/350°F. Grease and line 8 holes of a 12-hole (¾ cup/180ml) straight sided, loose-based mini cheese cake pan.

2 Combine ground hazelnuts, baking powder, sultanas and hazelnuts in a medium bowl.

3 Whisk honey, coconut oil, extract, mixed spice and eggs in a medium bowl until smooth. Pour honey mixture over dry ingredients; mix well. Fold in grated carrot and beetroot. Spoon mixture into holes.

4 Bake cakes for 30 minutes or until a skewer inserted in the centre comes out clean. Leave cakes in pan for 5 minutes before transferring to a wire rack to cool.

5 Meanwhile, make candied beetroot.

6 Serve cakes topped with candied beetroot and yoghurt.

candied beetroot Using a mandoline or V-slicer, cut beetroot into very thinly slices. Place slices in a medium saucepan with maple syrup; cook over medium heat for 10 minutes or until beetroot is candied.

prep + cook time 40 minutes **makes** 8

nutritional count per cake 35.9g total fat (8.7g saturated fat); 2651kJ (633 cal); 68.1g carbohydrate; 9.9g protein; 7g fibre

tip While the cakes themselves are dairy-free, if you serve them with the vanilla yoghurt, they are not.

KUMARA & COCONUT TARTS

WITH PECAN TOFFEE

1½ CUPS (180G) GROUND ALMONDS

⅓ CUP (50G) COCONUT FLOUR

2 TABLESPOONS TAPIOCA FLOUR

2 TABLESPOONS COCONUT SUGAR

1 TEASPOON GROUND GINGER

2 FREE-RANGE EGGS

⅓ CUP (80G) COCONUT OIL, MELTED

500G (1 POUND) KUMARA (ORANGE SWEET POTATO), CUT INTO 3CM (1¼-INCH) PIECES

1 TABLESPOON WATER

¾ CUP (180ML) COCONUT CREAM

2 FREE-RANGE EGGS, EXTRA

¼ CUP (60ML) PURE MAPLE SYRUP

1 TEASPOON MIXED SPICE

1 CUP (280G) COCONUT YOGHURT

PECAN PRALINE

¾ CUP (90G) PECAN HALVES

½ CUP (80G) COCONUT SUGAR

½ CUP (125ML) WATER

1 Preheat oven to 180°C/350°F. Grease six 10cm (4-inch) round flan tins with removable bases.

2 Process ground almonds, flours, coconut sugar and ginger in a food processor to combine. Add eggs and coconut oil, processing until just combined. Press mixture evenly over base and sides of tins. Place tins on an oven tray.

3 Bake for 10 minutes or until golden.

4 Meanwhile, place kumara and the water in a small microwave-safe bowl; cover with plastic wrap. Microwave on HIGH (100%) for 8 minutes or until tender. Drain; cool.

5 Blend or process kumara with coconut cream, extra eggs, maple syrup and mixed spice until smooth. Pour mixture into tart shells.

6 Bake tarts for 15 minutes until just set with a slight wobble in the centre. Turn oven off; cool in oven. Refrigerate for 2 hours.

7 Make pecan praline.

8 Just before serving, top tarts with yoghurt and praline.

pecan praline Spread nuts on a baking-paper-lined oven tray. Stir coconut sugar and the water in a small saucepan over medium-high heat, without boiling, until sugar dissolves. Bring to the boil; boil, uncovered, without stirring, for 6 minutes until it reaches hard crack stage (when a drizzle of syrup dropped into iced water turns into hard brittle shards). Pour toffee over nuts on tray, titling to spread into a thin even layer. Allow to cool and set. Break praline into pieces.

prep + cook time 45 minutes (+ cooling & refrigeration)

serves 6

nutritional count per serving 51.5g total fat (21.5g saturated fat); 3282kJ (784 cal); 62.1g carbohydrate; 18.4g protein; 9.7g fibre

tips Tarts can be made up to 2 days ahead; store, covered in the fridge. Top with yoghurt and praline before serving. Praline can be stored in an airtight container for up to 2 weeks.

I AM
GLUTEN FREE
PROTEIN RICH
DAIRY FREE

MIXED BERRY *And* COCONUT LAYER CAKE

6 FREE-RANGE EGGS

2 TEASPOONS VANILLA BEAN PASTE

¾ CUP (165G) MAPLE SUGAR

¼ CUP (60G) COCONUT OIL, MELTED

1½ CUPS (180G) GROUND ALMONDS

3 TEASPOONS GLUTEN-FREE BAKING POWDER

500G (1 POUND) COCONUT YOGHURT

125G (4 OUNCES) FRESH RASPBERRIES

125G (4 OUNCES) FRESH BLUEBERRIES

1 Preheat oven to 180°C/350°F. Grease and line two 20cm (8-inch) round cake pans with baking paper.

2 Beat eggs, paste and maple sugar in a small bowl with an electric mixer for 10 minutes or until light and creamy. Add coconut oil; beat for a further 3 minutes.

3 Transfer mixture to a large bowl; gently stir in ground almonds and baking powder. Spoon mixture evenly between pans.

4 Bake cakes, rotating pans halfway through cooking, for 25 minutes or until cakes spring back when lightly pressed with finger. Turn cakes immediately, top-side down, onto wire racks to cool.

5 Place one cake layer on serving plate; top with half the yoghurt and half the berries. Top with second cake, then remaining yoghurt and remaining berries.

prep + cook time 40 minutes (+ cooling) **serves** 6
nutritional count per serving 33.2g total fat (12.9g saturated fat); 2232kJ (533 cal); 41.5g carbohydrate; 17g protein; 4.4g fibre
tip Cake is best made and assembled on day of serving.

SIENNA CAKE CAN BE MADE UP TO 1 MONTH AHEAD.
STORE, IN AN AIRTIGHT CONTAINER, IN THE FRIDGE.

SIENNA CAKE

120G (4 OUNCES) BLANCHED ALMONDS, CHOPPED COARSELY

120G (4 OUNCES) SHELLED PISTACHIOS

⅓ CUP (50G) DRIED APRICOTS, CHOPPED

⅓ CUP (50G) GOLDEN RAISINS

⅓ CUP (50G) DRIED CHERRIES

⅓ CUP (50G) DRIED BLUEBERRIES

¼ CUP (40G) MIXED PEEL

½ CUP (60G) NATURAL GROUND ALMONDS

1 TEASPOON GROUND CINNAMON

½ TEASPOON GROUND NUTMEG

¼ CUP (12G) RAW CACAO POWDER

⅔ CUP (240G) HONEY

½ CUP (80G) COCONUT SUGAR

30G (1 OUNCE) BUTTER

1 TEASPOON VANILLA BEAN PASTE

RAW CACAO POWDER, EXTRA, TO SERVE

1 Preheat oven to 180°C/350°F. Grease and line a 20cm (8-inch) round shallow cake pan with baking paper.

2 Combine blanched almonds, pistachios, dried fruit and mixed peel in a large heatproof bowl. Combine ground almonds, cinnamon, nutmeg and cacao powder in a small bowl. Add ground almond mixture to fruit and nut mixture; mix well.

3 Stir honey, coconut sugar and butter in a small saucepan over medium heat for 3 minutes or until sugar dissolves and mixture starts to bubble. Remove from heat; stir in paste. Pour over dry mixture; quickly mix well. Spread mixture into pan; level surface with a spoon dipped in hot water.

4 Bake cake for 35 minutes or until a skewer inserted into the centre come out slightly sticky, but not wet. Leave in pan to cook completely. Wrap in foil. Stand overnight at room temperature. Serve dusted with extra cacao powder.

prep + cook time 45 minutes (+ cooling) **serves** 8
nutritional count per serving 22.5g total fat (3.2g saturated fat); 2076kJ (496 cal); 66.5g carbohydrate; 8.9g protein; 5.2g fibre

I AM

EGG FREE

HIGH IN CALCIUM

VITAMIN E

I AM
EGG FREE
HIGH FIBRE
VITAMIN C

SLOW-ROASTED ROSÉ *And* VANILLA
QUINCE GALETTE

3 MEDIUM QUINCE (1KG)

¼ CUP (90G) HONEY

3 CUPS (750ML) WATER

1½ CUPS (375ML) ROSÉ WINE

1 CINNAMON STICK

1 VANILLA BEAN, SPLIT LENGTHWAYS INTO THIRDS

6 SHEETS FILLO PASTRY

2 TABLESPOONS EXTRA VIRGIN OLIVE OIL

1 TEASPOON GROUND CINNAMON

⅓ CUP (75G) LOW GI CASTER (SUPERFINE) SUGAR

⅓ CUP (40G) GROUND ALMONDS

¼ CUP (40G) ROASTED ALMONDS, CHOPPED

1 CUP (280G) VANILLA BEAN GREEK-STYLE YOGHURT

1 Preheat oven to 150°C/300°F.

2 Peel quince; reserve half the peel. Cut quince into quarters, do not core.

3 Stir honey, the water, wine, cinnamon and vanilla in a large cast iron casserole or baking dish over medium heat until honey dissolves. Add quince and reserved peel, bring to the boil; cover with a piece of baking paper then cover tightly with foil, or a lid (make sure quince is submerged in the liquid).

4 Bake quince for 5 hours, turning twice, until quince are tender and deep red in colour. Leave quince in syrup to cool.

5 Remove quince from syrup with a slotted spoon. Cut cores from quince; cut each quarter in half lengthways. Strain syrup; reserve vanilla bean, discard peel. Reserve 2 cups (500ml) of the syrup. Return quince to remaining syrup; stand until required. Place reserved syrup in a saucepan over medium heat; simmer for 5 minutes or until thickened. Cool.

6 Preheat oven to 210°C/420°F. Grease a large oven tray; place tray in oven while heating.

7 Layer pastry sheets in alternate directions, on a large piece of baking paper, brushing each layer with some of the oil.

8 Combine cinnamon and sugar in a small bowl; reserve 2 tablespoons cinnamon sugar. Combine ground almonds with remaining cinnamon sugar. Sprinkle almond mixture over pastry leaving a 10cm (4-inch) border. Top with drained quince, fold edges of pastry over quince. Transfer galette, on baking paper, to preheated tray. Brush pastry with remaining oil; sprinkle pastry with reserved cinnamon sugar.

9 Bake galette for 20 minutes or until pastry is golden. Drizzle with reduced syrup, top with chopped almonds and reserved vanilla beans; serve with yoghurt.

prep + cook time 6 hours (+ cooling) **serves** 6
nutritional count per serving 16.4g total fat (3g saturated fat); 1985kJ (474 cal); 60.9g carbohydrate; 6.9g protein; 10.3g fibre
tip Quince can be prepared to the end of step 4, up to 3 days ahead; keep, covered, in the fridge.

GLOSSARY

AGAVE SYRUP from the agave plant; has a low GI, but that is due to the high percentage of fructose present, which may be harmful in large quantities.

ALLSPICE also known as pimento or jamaican pepper; so-named because it tastes like a combination of nutmeg, cumin, clove and cinnamon. Available whole or ground.

BAKING PAPER also called parchment paper or baking parchment – is a silicone-coated paper that is used for lining baking pans and oven trays so cooked food doesn't stick, making removal easy.

BAKING POWDER a raising agent consisting mainly of two parts cream of tartar to one part bicarbonate of soda (baking soda).

BARLEY a nutritious grain used in soups and stews. Hulled barley, the least processed, is high in fibre. Pearl barley has had the husk removed then been steamed and polished so that only the 'pearl' of the original grain remains, much the same as white rice.

BEANS

broad (fava) available dried, fresh, canned and frozen. Fresh should be peeled twice (discarding both the outer long green pod and the beige-green tough inner shell); the frozen beans have had their pods removed but the beige shell still needs removal.

butter cans labelled butter beans are, in fact, cannellini beans. Confusingly, it's also another name for lima beans, sold both dried and canned; a large beige bean with a mealy texture and mild taste.

cannellini a small white bean similar in appearance and flavour to other white beans (great northern, navy or haricot), all of which can be substituted for the other. Available dried or canned.

kidney medium-sized red bean, slightly floury in texture, yet sweet in flavour.

white a generic term we use for canned or dried cannellini, haricot, navy or great northern beans belonging to the same family, phaseolus vulgaris.

BEETROOT (BEETS) firm, round root vegetable.

BICARBONATE OF SODA (BAKING SODA) a raising agent.

BROCCOLINI a cross between broccoli and chinese kale; it has long asparagus-like stems with a long loose floret, both are edible. Resembles broccoli but is milder and sweeter in taste.

BUTTER use salted or unsalted (sweet) butter; 125g (4 ounces) is equal to one stick of butter.

BUTTERMILK originally the term given to the slightly sour liquid left after butter was churned from cream, today it is made from no-fat or low-fat milk to which specific bacterial cultures have been added. Despite its name, it is actually low in fat.

CAPERS grey-green buds of a warm climate shrub (usually Mediterranean), sold either dried and salted or pickled in a vinegar brine. Capers must be rinsed well before using.

CAPSICUM (BELL PEPPER) also called pepper. Comes in many colours: red, green, yellow, orange and purplish-black. Be sure to discard seeds and membranes before use.

CARDAMOM a spice native to India and used extensively in its cuisine; can be purchased in pod, seed or ground form. Has a distinctive aromatic, sweetly rich flavour.

CAVOLO NERO (TUSCAN CABBAGE) has long, narrow, wrinkled leaves and a rich and astringent, mild cabbage flavour. It doesn't lose its volume like silver beet or spinach when cooked, but it does need longer cooking.

CHEESE

goat's made from goat's milk, has an earthy, strong taste; available in both soft and firm textures, in various shapes and sizes, and sometimes rolled in ash or herbs.

haloumi a firm, cream-coloured sheep-milk cheese matured in brine; haloumi can be grilled or fried, briefly, without breaking down. Should be eaten while still warm as it becomes tough and rubbery on cooling.

pecorino the Italian generic name for cheeses made from sheep milk; hard, white to pale-yellow in colour. If you can't find it, use parmesan instead.

ricotta a soft, sweet, moist, white cow-milk cheese with a low fat content and a slightly grainy texture. The name roughly translates as 'cooked again' and refers to ricotta's manufacture from a whey that is itself a by-product of other cheese making.

CHICKPEAS (GARBANZO BEANS) an irregularly round, sandy-coloured legume. Has a firm texture even after cooking, a floury mouth-feel and robust nutty flavour; available canned or dried (soak for several hours in cold water before use).

CHILLI generally, the smaller the chilli, the hotter it is. Use rubber gloves when seeding and chopping fresh chillies as they can burn your skin. Removing seeds and membranes lessens the heat level.

CHOCOLATE, DARK (SEMI-SWEET) also called luxury chocolate; made of a high percentage of cocoa liquor and cocoa butter, and little added sugar. Dark chocolate is ideal for use in desserts and cakes.

CINNAMON available in pieces (called sticks or quills) and ground into powder; one of the world's most common spices.

COCOA POWDER also called unsweetened cocoa; cocoa beans (cacao seeds) that have been fermented, roasted, shelled, ground into powder then cleared of most of the fat content.

COCONUT

cream obtained commercially from the first pressing of the coconut flesh alone, without the addition of water; the second pressing (less rich) is sold as coconut milk. Available in cans and cartons at most supermarkets.

desiccated concentrated, dried, unsweetened and finely shredded coconut flesh.

flaked dried flaked coconut flesh.

milk not the liquid inside the fruit (coconut water), but the diluted liquid from the second pressing of the white flesh of a mature coconut. Available in cans and cartons at most supermarkets.

oil is extracted from the coconut flesh, so you don't get any of the fibre, protein or carbohydrates present in the whole coconut. The best quality is virgin coconut oil, which is the oil pressed from the dried coconut flesh, and doesn't include the use of solvents or other refining processes.

shredded thin strips of dried coconut.

sugar is not made from coconuts, but the sap of the blossoms of the coconut palm tree. The refined sap looks a little like raw or light brown sugar, and has a similar caramel flavour. It also has the same amount of kilojoules as regular white (granulated) sugar.

young are coconuts that are not fully mature. As a coconut ages, the amount of juice inside decreases, until it eventually disappears and is replaced by air.

CORIANDER (CILANTRO) also known as pak chee or chinese parsley; a bright-green leafy herb with a pungent flavour. Both stems and roots of coriander are also used in cooking; wash well before using. Also available ground or as seeds; these should not be substituted for fresh as the tastes are completely different.

CORNFLOUR (CORNSTARCH) available made from corn or wheat; used as a thickening agent in cooking.

COUSCOUS a fine, dehydrated, grain-like cereal product made from semolina; it swells to three or four times its original size when liquid is added. It is eaten like rice with a tagine, as a side dish or salad ingredient.

CREAM, POURING also called pure or fresh cream. It has no additives and contains a minimum fat content of 35%.

CUMIN also known as zeera or comino; has a spicy, nutty flavour.

DAIKON also called white radish; this long, white horseradish has a wonderful, sweet flavour. After peeling, eat it raw in salads or shredded as a garnish; also great when sliced or cubed and cooked in stir-fries and casseroles. The flesh is white but the skin can be either white or black; buy those that are firm and unwrinkled from Asian food shops.

DUKKAH an Egyptian specialty spice mixture made up of roasted nuts, seeds and an array of aromatic spices.

EGGPLANT also called aubergine. Ranging in size from tiny to very large and in colour from pale green to deep purple. Can also be purchased char-grilled, packed in oil, in jars.

FENNEL also known as finocchio or anise; a white to very pale green-white, firm, crisp, roundish vegetable about 8-12cm in diameter. The bulb has a slightly sweet, anise flavour but the leaves have a much stronger taste. Also the name of dried seeds having a licorice flavour.

FISH SAUCE also called nam pla or nuoc nam; made from pulverised salted fermented fish, most often anchovies. Has a pungent smell and strong taste, so use sparingly.

FLOUR

chickpea (besan) creamy yellow flour made from chickpeas and is very nutritious.

plain (all-purpose) a general all-purpose wheat flour.

rice very fine, almost powdery, gluten-free flour; made from ground white rice. Used in baking, as a thickener, and in some Asian noodles and desserts. Another variety, made from glutinous sweet rice, is used for chinese dumplings and rice paper.

self-raising plain flour sifted with baking powder in the proportion of 1 cup flour to 2 teaspoons baking powder.

wholemeal also known as wholewheat flour; milled with the wheat germ so is higher in fibre and more nutritional than plain flour.

FREEKEH is cracked roasted green wheat and can be found in some larger supermarkets, health food and specialty food stores.

GAI LAN also known as chinese broccoli, gai larn, kanah, gai lum and chinese kale; used more for its stems than its coarse leaves.

GARAM MASALA a blend of spices that includes cardamom, cinnamon, coriander, cloves, fennel and cumin. Black pepper and chilli can be added for heat.

GELATINE we use dried (powdered) gelatine; it's also available in sheet form called leaf gelatine. Three teaspoons of dried gelatine (8g or one sachet) is about the same as four gelatine leaves.

GINGER, PICKLED pink or red in colour, paper-thin shavings of ginger pickled in a mixture of vinegar, sugar and natural colouring. Available from Asian food shops.

HARISSA a Moroccan paste made from dried chillies, cumin, garlic, oil and caraway seeds. Available from Middle Eastern food shops and supermarkets.

KAFFIR LIME LEAVES also known as bai magrood. Aromatic leaves of a citrus tree; two glossy dark green leaves joined end to end, forming a rounded hourglass shape. A strip of fresh lime peel may be substituted for each kaffir lime leaf.

KUMARA (ORANGE SWEET POTATO) the Polynesian name of an orange-fleshed sweet potato often confused with yam.

LEMON GRASS a tall, clumping, lemon-smelling and -tasting, sharp-edged grass; the white part of the stem is used, finely chopped, in cooking.

LENTILS (red, brown, yellow) dried pulses often identified by and named after their colour; also known as dhal.

LSA A ground mixture of linseeds (L), sunflower seeds (S) and almonds (A); available from supermarkets and health food stores.

MAPLE SYRUP, PURE distilled from the sap of sugar maple trees found only in Canada and the USA. Maple-flavoured syrup or pancake syrup is not an adequate substitute for the real thing.

MIRIN a Japanese champagne-coloured cooking wine; made of glutinous rice and alcohol and used expressly for cooking. Should not be confused with sake.

MUSHROOMS, PORCINI also known as cèpes; the richest-flavoured mushrooms. Expensive, but because they're so strongly flavoured, only a small amount is required.

NORBU (MONK FRUIT SUGAR) monk fruit is a subtropical melon that contains a group of sweet tasting antioxidant compounds. Used as an alternative to cane sugar, as it has 96% fewer kilojoules and will not affect blood glucose or insulin levels.

OIL

coconut see Coconut

olive made from ripened olives. Extra virgin and virgin are the first and second press, respectively, of the olives; "light" refers to taste not fat levels.

peanut pressed from ground peanuts; most commonly used oil in Asian cooking because of its high smoke point (capacity to handle high heat without burning).

ONION

green (scallions) also called, incorrectly, shallot; an immature onion picked before the bulb has formed. Has a long, bright-green edible stalk.

shallots also called french or golden shallots or eschalots; small and brown-skinned.

OYSTER SAUCE Asian in origin, this thick, richly flavoured brown sauce is made from oysters and their brine, cooked with salt and soy sauce, and thickened with starches. Use as a condiment.

PERSIMMONS an autumnal fruit available in two varieties: an stringent one, eaten soft, and a non-astringent, or sweet, variety also known as fuji fruit.

POMEGRANATE dark-red, leathery-skinned fruit about the size of an orange filled with hundreds of seeds, each wrapped in an edible lucent-crimson pulp with a unique tangy sweet-sour flavour.

POMEGRANATE MOLASSES not to be confused with pomegranate syrup or grenadine; pomegranate molasses is thicker, browner and more concentrated in flavour – tart, sharp, slightly sweet and fruity. Available from Middle Eastern food stores or specialty food shops, and some supermarkets.

QUINOA pronounced keen-wa; is a gluten-free grain. It has a delicate, slightly nutty taste and chewy texture.

RHUBARB a plant with long, green-red stalks; becomes sweet and edible when cooked.

RICE, WILD BLEND a packaged blend of white long-grain rice and wild rice. With its dark brown, almost black grains, crunchy, resilient texture and smokey-like flavour, wild rice contrasts nicely with mild-tasting white rice. Perfect with fish, lentils, in pulaos or added to soups.

RICE MALT SYRUP also known as brown rice syrup or rice syrup; is made by cooking brown rice flour with enzymes to break down its starch into sugars from which the water is removed.

ROASTING/TOASTING desiccated coconut, pine nuts and sesame seeds roast more evenly if stirred over low heat in a heavy-based frying pan; their natural oils will help turn them golden brown. Remove from pan immediately. Nuts and dried coconut can be roasted in the oven to release their aromatic essential oils. Spread them evenly onto an oven tray then roast at 180°C/350°F for about 5 minutes.

SAFFRON available ground or in strands; imparts a yellow-orange colour to food once infused. The quality can vary greatly; the best is the most expensive spice in the world.

SILVER BEET also called swiss chard; mistakenly called spinach.

SOY SAUCE made from fermented soya beans. Several variations are available in most supermarkets and Asian food stores. We use japanese soy sauce unless stated otherwise.

SPINACH also called english spinach and, incorrectly, silver beet.

STAR ANISE dried star-shaped pod with an astringent aniseed flavour; used to flavour stocks and marinades. Available whole and ground, it is an essential ingredient in five-spice powder.

STERLISING JARS it's important the jars be as clean as possible; make sure your hands, the preparation area, tea towels and cloths etc, are clean, too. The aim is to finish sterilising the jars and lids at the same time the preserve is ready to be bottled; the hot preserve should be bottled into hot, dry clean jars. Jars that aren't sterilised properly can cause deterioration of the preserves during storage. Always start with cleaned washed jars and lids, then follow one of these methods:

(1) Put jars and lids through the hottest cycle of a dishwasher without using any detergent.

(2) Lie jars down in a boiler with the lids, cover them with cold water then cover the boiler with a lid. Bring the water to the boil over a high heat and boil the jars for 20 minutes.

(3) Stand jars upright, without touching each other, on a wooden board on the lowest shelf in the oven. Turn the oven to the lowest possible temperature; leave jars to heat for 30 minutes.

Remove the jars from the oven or dishwasher with a towel, or from the boiling water with tongs and rubber-gloved hands; the water will evaporate from hot wet jars quite quickly. Stand jars upright and not touching on a wooden board, or a bench covered with a towel to protect and insulate the bench. Fill the jars as directed in the recipe; secure the lids tightly, holding jars firmly with a towel or an oven mitt. Leave at room temperature to cool before storing.

SUGAR

brown very soft, finely granulated sugar retaining molasses for its characteristic colour and flavour.

caster (superfine) finely granulated table sugar.

coconut see Coconut

palm also called nam tan pip, jaggery, jawa or gula melaka; made from the sap of the sugar palm tree. Light brown to black in colour and usually sold in rock-hard cakes; use brown sugar if unavailable.

SUMAC a purple-red, astringent spice ground from berries growing on shrubs flourishing wild around the Mediterranean; adds a tart, lemony flavour to food. Available from major supermarkets.

TAHINI a rich, sesame-seed paste.

TAMARI a thick, dark soy sauce made mainly from soya beans, but without the wheat used in most standard soy sauces.

VANILLA

bean dried, long, thin pod from a tropical golden orchid; the minuscule black seeds inside the bean impart a luscious flavour in baking and desserts.

extract obtained from vanilla beans infused in water; a non-alcoholic version of essence

paste made from vanilla beans and contains real seeds. Is highly concentrated: 1 teaspoon replaces a whole vanilla bean. Found in most supermarkets in the baking section.

WATERCRESS one of the cress family, a large group of peppery greens. Highly perishable, so must be used as soon as possible after purchase. It has an exceptionally high vitamin K content, which is great for eye health, and is an excellent source of calcium.

WOMBOK (NAPA CABBAGE) also known as peking or chinese cabbage. Elongated in shape with pale green, crinkly leaves.

YEAST (dried and fresh), a raising agent used in dough making. Granular (7g sachets) and fresh compressed (20g blocks) yeast can almost always be substituted for the other.

YOGHURT, GREEK-STYLE plain yoghurt strained in a cloth (muslin) to remove the whey and to give it a creamy consistency.

CONVERSION CHART

MEASURES

One Australian metric measuring cup holds approximately 250ml; one Australian metric tablespoon holds 20ml; one Australian metric teaspoon holds 5ml.

The difference between one country's measuring cups and another's is within a two- or three-teaspoon variance, and will not affect your cooking results.
North America, New Zealand and the United Kingdom use a 15ml tablespoon.

All cup and spoon measurements are level. The most accurate way of measuring dry ingredients is to weigh them. When measuring liquids, use a clear glass or plastic jug with the metric markings.

The imperial measurements used in these recipes are approximate only. Measurements for cake pans are approximate only. Using same-shaped cake pans of a similar size should not affect the outcome of your baking. We measure the inside top of the cake pan to determine sizes.

We use large eggs with an average weight of 60g.

DRY MEASURES

METRIC	IMPERIAL
15G	½OZ
30G	1OZ
60G	2OZ
90G	3OZ
125G	4OZ (¼LB)
155G	5OZ
185G	6OZ
220G	7OZ
250G	8OZ (½LB)
280G	9OZ
315G	10OZ
345G	11OZ
375G	12OZ (¾LB)
410G	13OZ
440G	14OZ
470G	15OZ
500G	16OZ (1LB)
750G	24OZ (1½LB)
1KG	32OZ (2LB)

LIQUID MEASURES

METRIC	IMPERIAL
30ML	1 FLUID OZ
60ML	2 FLUID OZ
100ML	3 FLUID OZ
125ML	4 FLUID OZ
150ML	5 FLUID OZ
190ML	6 FLUID OZ
250ML	8 FLUID OZ
300ML	10 FLUID OZ
500ML	16 FLUID OZ
600ML	20 FLUID OZ
1000ML (1 LITRE)	1¾ PINTS

LENGTH MEASURES

METRIC	IMPERIAL
3MM	⅛IN
6MM	¼IN
1CM	½IN
2CM	¾IN
2.5CM	1IN
5CM	2IN
6CM	2½IN
8CM	3IN
10CM	4IN
13CM	5IN
15CM	6IN
18CM	7IN
20CM	8IN
22CM	9IN
25CM	10IN
28CM	11IN
30CM	12IN (1FT)

OVEN TEMPERATURES

The oven temperatures in this book are for conventional ovens;
if you have a fan-forced oven, decrease the temperature by 10-20 degrees.

	°C (CELSIUS)	°F (FAHRENHEIT)
VERY SLOW	120	250
SLOW	150	300
MODERATELY SLOW	160	325
MODERATE	180	350
MODERATELY HOT	200	400
HOT	220	425
VERY HOT	240	475

INDEX